CW00820979

This book and its related websites: *www.markcarmichael.com* and *theintelligentexit.com* (and co.uk) have been prepared for general information on matters of interest only, and do not constitute professional advice on facts and circumstances specific to any person or company. You should not act upon the information contained in this publication without obtaining specific professional advice. No representation or warranty (express or implied) is given as to the accuracy or completeness of the information contained in this publication. The author, any of his related entities and their respective employees, consultants, agents or otherwise shall not be responsible for any loss sustained by any person who relies on this publication.

AUTHOR'S NOTE ON THE 2ND EDITION OF THE INTELLIGENT EXIT

Since first publishing this book in 2017, I've been thrilled to see how many people it has helped around the world. I've "connected" with nearly 10,000 entrepreneurs in these pages, helping them make better, more informed decisions about how to sell their businesses most effectively.

In this 2nd Edition of The Intelligent Exit, I include additional insights and lessons learned during my continuing journey in which I assist business owners globally in their own respective business exits. I've also updated the relevant data points and statistics used throughout to ensure their accuracy and relevance. And finally, due to the surprisingly positive feedback from readers who took up the offer extended in the 1st edition to engage directly with me, I've extended this same courtesy in this latest edition; you are quite welcome to reach out to me and my team if we can be of any assistance to you. **You can always email me at *ExitSupport@markcarmichael.com*.** I'd love to hear from you and we always respond to reader's requests.

In 2021, I created and launched **The Exit Academy**, an 11 ½ hour online, on-demand video course on how to develop, implement and execute the most effective strategy for selling your business. It's an extension of this book and is, to our knowledge, the most comprehensive video course in the world on this topic. It goes in depth on each stage of the selling process, following my Selling-Your-Business Roadmap™ which is designed to empower, educate, and motivate entrepreneurs globally on achieving their best possible exit.

Reading this book and/or participating in The Exit Academy video course (*www.markcarmichael.com/exit-academy*) is going to profoundly impact how you approach the sale of your business. As you'll see in the following pages, the advice given in this book has attracted the praise of several notable entrepreneurs, investors, CEO coaches and academics alike.

After reading this book and/or completing The Exit Academy, you'll be more prepared and educated on the issue of selling your business than 99 percent of the business owners that I've encountered in the last 15 years. Literally.

Remember, this is your exit; it's the launching pad for life's next chapters. Take control. Be informed. Be empowered.

No business is guaranteed to sell. However, if you develop the necessary understanding on the selling-your-business journey and develop the clarity, confidence, and motivation to direct your exit efforts, then the probability of your successful exit is dramatically improved. You can count on this.

Realizing a successful exit is important not just from a financial perspective, but also from the perspective of your employees, fellow co-shareholders, your company, the community in which your business exists and more.

As a result of this, the path you choose in your exit is for most, one of life's most important decisions. It pays, therefore, to know the rules before you get in the game so that you can develop, implement and execute the most effective exit strategy possible.

Learn more at *www.markcarmichael.com.*

THE INTELLIGENT EXIT

The Business Owner's Guide to a Winning Strategy
for Selling Your Company

SECOND EDITION

by Mark Carmichael

PAPERBOY
PUBLISHING

Published by Paperboy Publishers

ISBN: 978-94-92806-03-1

cover photograph © ra2studio/shutterstock.com

www.paperboypublishers.com

TABLE OF CONTENTS

For Marije, Maximilian, Mason and Amelia.

And to the road less traveled.

WHAT PEOPLE SAY ABOUT *THE INTELLIGENT EXIT*

"*The Intelligent Exit* provides the framework of value-added strategies and comprehensive tools to sell businesses more profitably. Mark's perspective on the sell-side process is highly unique and will be of significant value to any shareholder, CEO, founder or otherwise who is looking to sell their business. As an active investor myself in numerous companies over the years, I am certain that the approach to selling businesses that Mark has developed and outlines in his book will make a positive difference to any business owner's sell-side strategy. Any entrepreneur looking to strengthen his/her knowledge on the principles of a successful selling strategy should get to know Mark and his methodology."

Igor Sill, Silicon Valley VC and early-stage investor in Salesforce.com, Siebel Systems (Oracle), Weblogic, Square, RedOwl, NetGravity and Threatmetrix. Current/past Advisory Board Member of: Salesforce.com, IMF, Strawberry Creek Ventures (UC Berkeley) and Red Herring Communications.

"Carmichael's book embodies much wisdom and much experience in direct, accessible language. I taught Mark at Oxford University in 2006 and have watched with appreciation his transitions from serial entrepreneur to investment banker and now, author and teacher. *The Intelligent Exit* consolidates his diverse successes into a primer for action that speaks directly to entrepreneurs who want to chart the most effective path to exit. The guidance comes in a down-to-earth tone and with common-sense advice easy to understand and implement."

Marc Ventresca Ph.D., Professor of Strategic Management at the Saïd Business School; Research affiliations at the Oxford Institute for Science, Innovation and Society, the Center for International Security and Cooperation at Stanford University, and the Stanford Center for Innovation and Communication, the Center for Organizational Research at the University of California.

"VanMoof has become one of the most successful e-bike brands in the world. As a co-founder, it's important to have others around me who challenge assumptions and offer fresh perspectives and strategies. Mark is absolutely that type of individual. He understands that my company means the world to me and serves as great sparring partner on all matters related to our corporate finance needs. He's down to earth, passionate, very creative and seems to know everyone."

Taco Carlier, Co-founder and CEO, VanMoof (www.vanmoof.com).
VanMoof is one of the world's leading e-bike design & manufacturers.

"Mark's approach to marketing and selling investment opportunities is the most comprehensive and international I've come across and is part of the reason why previous businesses and Formula 1 race teams I've been involved with have used Mark and his team at STS to deliver the results we were seeking. The tactics and methodologies they employ are far greater than any other investment banker we've come across and he and his team are great people to work with."

*Mark Preston, Team Principal of Formula E Champions, Team Techeetah, CEO of
StreetDrone, former Team Principal of Super Aguri Formula 1 Team*

"*The Intelligent Exit* is a must-read for business owners big and small, as it addresses an issue that most entrepreneurs struggle with or fail all together on: educating themselves before they initiate the process of selling their business. This book would have been of enormous benefit to several business owners I've come across over the years and is a resource I will gladly recommend in the future when the situation arises. Most M&A books focus on the buyer in the M&A process. Mark's book fills a gap in the marketplace by focusing on what matters most to the seller to ensure the most successful outcome."

*Tim Galpin, Ph.D. is a best-selling author, Senior Lecturer of Strategy & Innovation,
Academic Director of the MBA Program at University of Oxford,
and a consultant to boards and senior management*

FOREWORD

I first met Mark Carmichael in the Gobi Desert in China in 2006. We were both competing in a 250-kilometer, six-day, self-supported race across one of the driest and most remote places on the planet which both of us foolishly considered ourselves fit enough to enter. I remember meeting Mark at one of the checkpoints and we immediately connected. Within minutes, we realized we had both studied at the Saïd Business School of Oxford University only a few years apart, knew the same professors and had lived within 10 minutes of each other in England. Here we were, in the middle of absolutely nowhere, a Canadian and an American, recognizing what a small world we truly live in.

Three weeks later, I found myself sitting with Mark at his home along the banks of the Thames River, in Oxfordshire, talking about our shared pas- sions: entrepreneurship, philanthropy, marketing and deal-making. Two days later, we decided to embark upon a business partnership and STS Capital Partners UK was born. I'm proud to say that since meeting one another in 2006, we have both grown as business partners and friends. We've shared family holidays together and have spent many late nights working on closing deals together.

So, when Mark asked me to write the foreword to his book, I said yes with pleasure and without hesitation. This book will empower entrepreneurs with the clarity, direction and confidence that is so often dangerously absent at the beginning stages when a business owner is considering the sale his/her business. For most, selling a business is a new experience. And given that it is often one of life's most significant financial transactions, it pays to invest in developing the right understandings and framework from the outset that will prepare you for making higher quality decisions throughout your own exit journey.

As the founder and chairman of STS Capital Partners International, I have had the privilege to advise on more than $40 billion worth of transactions since 2003. You can't be involved in that many transactions without making some profound observations about the patterns that surface amongst entrepreneurs seeking to sell. One of the most regrettable—and avoidable—is that which sees entrepreneur after entrepreneur commence their exit journey without the necessary understanding that can make the difference between success and failure when selling a business.

The Intelligent Exit will greatly assist you in this regard.

Today, Mark has evolved as a global thought leader in the M&A space. *The Intelligent Exit* has received international acclaim in the category of Best Business Book and earned Mark the prestigious recognition as the **International M&A Thought Leader of the Year** (runner-up) by the Association of M&A Advisors. Today, he is a regular speaker at global CEO and entrepreneur events, as well as a regular guest speaker to Executive Education and MBA classes at Oxford University. I've seen first-hand how his down-to-earth approach to providing guidance and counsel has assisted so many entrepreneurs, CEOs, investors and private banks seeking to learn more about Mark's highly regarded approach to selling businesses. For those readers who are members of Young Presidents' Organization (YPO), you may already be one of the thousands of YPO members who have who have heard Mark speak at YPO events in Mauritius, Lebanon, Rome, London or various other events he's spoken at in recent years.

After more than 18 years of assisting entrepreneurs on the sale of their businesses, I'm certain that this book will resonate and add value to so many entrepreneurs as they contemplate their own exit strategies. The international feedback that Mark has received on his book from entrepreneurs, CEOs and shareholders alike over the past 4 years overwhelmingly supports this. The practical advice found within this book will resonate with every business owner. The conversational tone and pragmatic guidance that this book provides will equip you with meaningful insights, clarity and direction that will assist you in your own journey.

Robert C. Follows
Founding Chairman, STS Capital Partners International

INTRODUCTION

"I have found that all ugly things are made by those who strive to make something beautiful, and that all beautiful things are made by those who strive to make something useful."

– Oscar Wilde

I have always been driven by a fundamental belief: be useful.

Being useful is rewarding. When you help others, you also help yourself. Being useful makes us happier because the act of usefulness ensures that nothing we are doing is wasted. This form of generosity is deeply gratifying, especially if you have an entrepreneurial mind-set; if it is appropriately channelled, you can improve the lives of many who may find your experience and advice to be of significant benefit.

There are countless ways to be useful, but two in particular have always stood out:

- Share knowledge
- Solve a problem

I look around my professional landscape and see enormous need among my fellow entrepreneurs as it relates to the complex and emotionally daunting task of selling their businesses. Over the last 15 years, I have encountered and observed countless entrepreneurs who have failed in their attempts to successfully sell their companies; or worse, who completely failed to sell at all. In many instances, I genuinely believe that this did not need to be the case. And I know this all too well, as when I first set out to sell my first business some 25 years ago, I too found myself included among the disappointed. That painful process took its toll on me in ways that even today, are still hard to recount. An experience like that leaves an indelible impression and changes your perceptions in many ways.

Subsequently, I felt compelled to share the knowledge and experience I've developed in advising entrepreneurs around the world for the last 15 years about how they can navigate their uncharted waters. By first learning the "rules" of the exit process—and understanding the selling-your-business journey and how businesses are most effectively sold in today's world, business owners are able to empower themselves with the clarity, knowledge and confidence to develop, implement and execute the most effective strategies that will produce the highest probability of an extraordinary exit. I hope to help those with whom I have much in common to understand the beginning-to-end exit process so that they can then plot the right course to success. I am fortunate to have such an opportunity to be useful.

That's why I wrote this book.

I am a mergers-and-acquisitions (M&A) advisor. Most people don't know what M&A advisors or investment bankers actually do (different title, but in the context of M&A, essentially the same job). In the simplest terms, as an M&A advisor, I help the owners of privately-held companies around the world sell all or part of their businesses under terms that are the most successful for them. What "successful" means varies with every owner. My colleagues and I work with these business owners to help define and clarify what that word "success" means to them, and then help them to achieve it. I tell people "we are in the sales and marketing business, with a sophisticated understanding of entrepreneurialism, negotiation and corporate finance."

Most people in the investment banking world don't like to explain things in simple terms. They often wrap what they do in fancy, daunting language to make them seem more intelligent or important, and to make you feel dumb. They want you to believe you need them more than they need you. While that tactic may have worked in the 1980's, today that language often backfires with potential clients, who don't understand it and feel intimidated or stupid as a result. Who wants to work with someone who throws around arcane and unfamiliar terms? Who wants to be made to feel uninformed, even stupid, about their own company?

I favor a different approach. Whenever I have the opportunity to explain the mergers-and-acquisition process to a business owner, I illustrate my work in their terms—the terms of entrepreneurs. After 30+ years of building my own companies around the world, I find it more natural to speak in this manner. Rather than make myself feel important, I work to make myself useful.

I had that opportunity a few years back with the owner of a hotel business in England. Thinking about selling his company, he had previously arranged a preliminary meeting with a team from a leading global investment bank. The trio that showed up was, as he put it, "a bunch of 21-year-olds in grey suits and red ties." They proceeded, he said, to "make me feel stupid about my own business." He was so put off by the whole experience that he never proceeded with the sale.

We met two years later. We spoke as one entrepreneur to another over a pizza in Brighton, England. I put in plain words what an M&A advisor does, how it's done, and why it's done that way. I omitted the sales pitch. Instead, we had an open, unbiased discussion about the issues he needed to address and consider as they related to selling his business. "This is exactly what I've been looking for," he said. "Someone who speaks my language, who understands my issues and concerns regarding maximizing my exit, who knows what I'm after and sees my business from the buyer's perspective. Someone who appreciates that I don't have a clue as to how to sell my business. I certainly know my business inside and out—but I don't know how to sell it."

He then leaned across the table and said, "You know, if I had come across you guys two years ago, I'd probably be retired right now."

Business owners discover that my interactions with them are very down-to-earth, and that as a fellow entrepreneur I have a great deal in common with them. I get them. More importantly, we get each other. Often, after a half an hour or so of talk over a cup of coffee or a beer, my new acquaintance will say some version of: "I wish I'd had this conversation years ago." And that's the ultimate result for me. Whether that discussion leads to my getting a new client or not, I've added value. I've helped the other person to see a clearer path forward; an increased sense of "I can do this."

They're more enthusiastic and confident on the matter of selling their business now. There's a sparkle in their eye as they begin to see that the prospect of selling their business may not be a dot on the distant, "some-day" horizon, but rather something much more real—much sooner than "someday." They're motivated. They feel empowered. They want to know what steps to take next.

This book is my way to "have this conversation" with many more business owners than I can meet face-to-face. I sat down at the keyboard with a particular mindset. I run a mergers-and-acquisitions advisory firm, and of course, if we're a match, I would love to have you as a client. But that's not what this is about. I have seen an abundance of self-serving "brochures" posing as books in this arena. (It's funny how the answers you get are contingent upon whom you ask, isn't it?) I'm explaining my bias here because I want you to understand where I'm coming from, and to know that my intent is to offer you advice that is as straightforward and unbiased as I can manage. My hope is that this book will feel to you like a conversation over a cup of coffee, where we can look each other in the eye and you know that what you're hearing—or reading—is solid, actionable advice.

Since first publishing *The Intelligent Exit* in 2017, I've gone on to expand this "conversation" through the development of The Exit Academy (*markcarmichael.com/exit-academy*), an online, on-demand video training course on the same topic of how to develop, implement and execute the most effective strategy for selling your business. Across 11 ½ hours of video content, I cover the various aspects of selling your business that every business owner needs to be familiar with so that they can embark upon their own exit journey with the knowledge, confidence, conviction, clarity and sense of empowerment that every business needs to possess before they initiate one of life's most meaningful financial and emotional transactions.

If I achieve my goal of providing you with genuine advice, then I will have increased my usefulness exponentially, and this book will have been a success.

CHAPTER 1

THE INTELLIGENT EXIT

"It is not enough to do your best;
you must first know what to do, and THEN do your best."

—W. Edwards Deming

The point of this book is not to convince you to sell your business. Instead, I want to arm you with the right conceptual framework, structure, and know-how to think about *how* to sell your business in a manner that maximizes your chance for a successful exit, however you define that. It's my objective to ensure you know the rules of the game beforehand so that you can perform to the best of your ability. Knowing what to do and how to do it is half the battle. By the time you finish this book, you'll have a solid understanding of the steps to take, when to take them, and how to ensure the highest probability of the successful sale of your business.

At the outset, one of the most important things for you to learn is how early you can go wrong in this process. Many business owners make mistakes before they even realize they are in a position to make mistakes.

What am I talking about? There are two key considerations to bear in mind as you begin to think about selling.

The first is this: when you begin to explore the idea of selling your company, who you ask for advice and information, the questions you ask and in what order you ask them, can have a decisive impact on the overall success in selling your business.

Yet how would most people know that?

They wouldn't.

Let me elaborate. If you decided to explore selling your business today, who is the first professional advisor you would call to discuss it? Your accountant? Your lawyer? An investment banker?

No matter what your answer is, without possessing the knowledge of how businesses are bought and sold in today's world, there is a reasonable-to-high probability that your first call can set you on the wrong trajectory in your exit process.

Yet you may be thinking: "But I know and trust these people—why wouldn't I ask for their advice?" It's a valid question, to which there is a valid response.

To answer that question, let's look at this from a slightly different perspective. Would you ask your family doctor to fit your child for braces? Of course not—you'd ask an orthodontist. They both have medical training, but the orthodontist has a very particular specialty. It's the same with business professionals. Most legal firms, for instance, do not have the relevant internal resources or expertise required to value a company, nor do they have the in-house experience in marketing a business to investors, negotiating with multiple buyers and, ultimately, closing the sale with the best buyer.

Although some accounting and law firms have M&A departments to assist clients, they are relatively few and far between. Thus, your lawyer may be very good at providing the legal advice required to run your company, but in most cases, they don't have the tools, knowledge, and experience to devise, implement, and execute a strategy to *sell* your company optimally. Doing that is specialists' work, and it's simply not what most legal firms are set up to do.

That's a key distinction—"optimally." Some law firms, accountants, and business coaches may be able to help you sell it. But can they help you get the best deal, on the best terms, for your definition of success? And how would you even know?

Additionally, do you have complete confidence that they will tell you that they are *not* the best choice to help you with a sale? Because there's the rub—the phone call in which you say, "I'm thinking about selling the company," potentially represents a big fee for that lawyer or accountant. Their advice, however well intended, is likely to be influenced by that realization. They may be happy to help, but they may not be the best equipped to help. This immediately puts you at risk of engaging in a subpar deal that may leave millions of dollars on the table—or may not close at all. Yet many business owners don't perceive this risk in time—or ever.

Several years back, I saw a perfect example of this play out.

I know a London entrepreneur who had a small but very successful logistics company. His annual revenue was £10 million, and his earnings before interest, taxes, depreciation and amortization (EBITDA) were £1.5 million. His company was a unique offering, and my team knew it would be attractive to a number of strategic investors—that is, buyers who would want the company not simply for its cash flow, but also because of the various synergies and unique differentiators that the business posed to a new owner.

This gentleman didn't work with us, or with any other M&A advisor. Instead, he asked his accountant—with whom he had worked for 20 years—to sell the business. That accountant approached a handful of local logistics companies and accepted the first—and apparently only—offer he received. Although he probably didn't intend to, he structured a terrible deal for the owner that required him to earn out 50% of the purchase price over a 24-month period by achieving certain performance targets. The owner, presented with this deal, accepted a sales price of slightly more than £5 million.

When the owner told me about the deal, I didn't have the heart to say that he almost certainly had left a large pile of cash on the table. How large? After the terms of the deal become public knowledge (the accountant created a case study that he uploaded to his website), I had the chance to speak with two strategic buyers who knew the business and would have been interested in the deal. One disbelieving CEO said that he felt the company could have sold for £10–12 million. "Ten million pounds represents less than seven times EBITDA," he told me "I think we would have taken that deal in a second."

That entrepreneur had been shafted. And he didn't even know it.

The truth is most businesses sell for less than they should. If you think about it for a moment, this makes intuitive sense. Whatever your business is, if you're reading this book I am confident you're good at running that business. You have spent years—if not a lifetime—mastering the ins and outs of your field. You are demonstrably an expert in producing and providing the goods or services you think about every day. Yet I am also confident that you almost certainly don't know how to sell the very thing you have built over the years with the same eagle eye for the best deal. How could you? Unless you are a serial entrepreneur with a string of successful exits behind you, when would you have had the opportunity to learn?

Entrepreneurs spend their lives focused on running—and growing—their companies. The very expertise that they have developed in their fields, though, can blind them to the fact that they are not expert in executing what is, for most, the biggest, most important transaction of their professional lives: the sale of their company.

This book will help you avoid the pitfalls of so many others before you who have made this very costly mistake. No single book is ever going to make you an expert, but armed with the right framework, you will be empowered to chart the course to successfully execute the sale of your business for the right price, to the right party, and on the right terms.

＊＊

The second key consideration to remember as you consider selling all or part of your business is that it is a deeply emotional experience. We often like to think of business in terms of hard numbers and hard-nosed decision-making. Selling your company involves those elements, of course. But for many, the most important element is emotional. You are putting a price on, and parting with, something you made through years of toil. Your business likely has been the focus of your life for a long, long time. Many owners don't anticipate and/or know how to manage the emotional roller coaster associated with selling. They shy away from thinking deeply about what they want and why they want it. They may end up in a reactive, rather than proactive position, missing opportunities or failing to control events to effect the best outcome.

The solution, as in so many areas of our lives, is knowledge combined with execution. I am gratified that you are beginning with this book, because that means I have the opportunity to equip you with knowledge and set you up to take action.

＊＊

Entrepreneurs are cut from a different cloth—I should know. Long before I became an investment banker, I discovered my entrepreneurial drive. In 1990, when my classmates at Syracuse University (Utica College campus) were scrambling to assemble their resumes and honing their interview skills, I was creating my own, less-travelled path. After graduation,

I found myself in Luxembourg, working for Peugeot and playing basketball in that tiny country's professional basketball league (yes, you've never heard of it). I was a 21-year-old who had never left the East Coast of America prior to landing in northern Europe. My first trip abroad opened my mind to a wider world of opportunities.

Playing professional basketball in Europe was a means to an end—a way to see the world and gain life experience. Since we trained in the evenings and played most games on the weekends, my days were largely open, so I secured a role with Peugeot, overseeing the importation of vehicles from France and securing the requisite government approvals before they were delivered to dealer showrooms throughout Luxembourg. Although the forms were entirely in French, a language of which I spoke precisely four words at the time, I developed a system to ensure full compliance. I hired a team of six, and worked out an aggressive commission structure in which these six could earn far more money than they had been. Then I sat back and watched the money roll in.

It was nearly 200 bucks a week.

Because the entrepreneurial itch needs regular scratching, I also started a security services business called Pro-Tect, which offered doorman services to pubs and bars in Luxembourg. (Hey, I was 21.) I recruited other American basketball players as my hired thugs. My rate was modest: $50 per guy per night, plus all the beer we could drink. What could go wrong?

You take a lot of risks as an entrepreneur, and at Pro-Tect they were mostly physical. On a cold February night at a bar named after a fish (The Beckleck), I refused entry to a group of undesirables who subsequently pummeled me. I ended up in a snowy Luxembourg bush, bleeding profusely and realizing I'd just eaten a big piece of humble pie.

All in all, in addition to the salary I was earning playing basketball, I was taking in a supplemental personal fortune that equated to about $400 a week from my entrepreneurial endeavors, but I loved it. In many ways, I felt a greater sense of fulfilment related to this income stream than I did to my basketball salary. My early twenties marked the start of a lifelong fascination with all opportunities entrepreneurial.

Over the next 23 years, as a result of the desire to forge my own entrepreneurial path, I was fortunate enough to live around the world, settling in Perth and Sydney, Northern Ireland, the United States, Oxford (where I received my MBA at the University of Oxford, Christ Church College), and finally Amsterdam, where I have lived since 2012. Along the way, I always found unique opportunities to add value and expand my skill set and experience. I consulted for John Deere and Coca-Cola. I started a data-driven marketing agency that merged with another small firm to become one of the largest privately owned agencies in Australia. I created a European manufacturing company that produced a patented roofing system. After getting my graduate degree at Oxford, I had a stint as European CEO for a New Zealand software company and consulted for two family offices and a Formula One team. Eventually, I circled back to database marketing, developing for ScottishPower, one of the most successful integrated multimedia direct marketing campaigns ever in the UK.

During this period I invested in, and divested of, companies that I had created, and I'll be frank: I did not always achieve an optimal exit. Today, after more than 15 years as an M&A advisor, I look back at my own previous exits all those years ago and see the patently obvious mistakes I made. It is only from my current vantage point, with the experience of scores of M&A transactions I've been directly involved with around the world, that I appreciate how blissfully unaware I was about what it takes to sell a company the right way. I did exactly what I hope you will *not* do: I was naïve and egotistical enough to think I could handle a sale myself. Inevitably, there were disappointing outcomes along the way.

Thus, when I considered writing this book, I chose to write what I wish I had read back then. Selling your business is a long, complex, personal and often arduous journey. It's easy to hit potholes and take wrong turns along the way. Without a good guide, what starts out as a hopeful undertaking can end in wasted time and money, a lower sales price than you want, unattractive deal terms, or outright failure to sell. This book is the guide I wish I had. It would have made all the difference to me.

* * *

After half a lifetime of developing and establishing my own companies, I relate to the entrepreneurs we help as peers. When one client told me how financial stress had nearly led him to kill himself, I genuinely knew what he meant. When another said his focus on his business had cost him his marriage, I understood that, too. The list of common experiences shared by entrepreneurs is lengthy.

A conversation among entrepreneurs is like a conversation among aircraft pilots—they have their own language. Sure, corporate guys may understand flight, but they're more like passengers in comparison. Entrepreneurs put it all at risk. We have been there, seen it all, and endured the highs and lows. We know what it's like to post a record annual profit, and what it's like to win industry awards. We also know the gut grind of wondering how you're going to make payroll next week, and the pain of letting an employee go. We know personally that there is a family behind that individual, relying on that paycheck.

We've put our personal wealth on the line, we've signed our houses as collateral against the much-needed bank loan, we've had employees stolen away and we've had employees steal. We've had honest business partners and we've been betrayed by those we trusted. We've borrowed from friends, family, and fools; we've dealt with venture capitalists and private equity investors; and we've heard numerous rejections before that long awaited "yes" from the investor who finally embraced our vision.

As entrepreneurs, we hold on to the notion that it's never too late to start living a dream. We see opportunity where others see impossibility. We take risks. We believe that anything is possible. We try. We create jobs. We believe in something bigger than ourselves. We're determined. We're focused. We're committed to fulfilling our entrepreneurial vision. We ask questions. We learn each day. We never lose that pure wonder and curiosity that you see in children. We believe that obstacles, turbulence, and failure lead to opportunities for success and achievement. We know from experience that what doesn't kill us only makes us stronger.

This is who we are. It's what we do. It's how we're wired. It shapes the way we see the world around us. And if you are an entrepreneur, then you know that only another entrepreneur can truly understand your experience.

**

The sale of your company is likely the most significant transaction of your business career. You and your family, perhaps also other investors, have spent a long time building up to this moment. You've reinvested profits, forgoing short-term rewards to expand, to improve, to ensure the longevity of the firm for you and your staff. You've sacrificed to get to this point. You have created value. And now you intend to harvest it.

In the following pages we'll explore the key phases that are part of any successful sale, written from the perspective of an entrepreneur first, an investment banker second. It is my sincere hope that this blend of entrepreneur and investment banker perspectives will result in an informative, relatable guide that will expand your understanding and confidence as you consider the sale of your business. In any event, I'd be grateful to hear your feedback, good or bad, anytime at ***mcarmichael@stscapital.com*** or ***ExitSupport@markcarmichael.com***.

The phases we'll discuss are:

- Valuation
- Exit Planning
- Hiring an M&A Advisor
- Forming Your Deal Team
- Pre-marketing and Pre-sales
- Marketing and Selling
- Exclusivity and Due Diligence
- Earn-Outs
- Closing
- Post-Sale Life

There's a lot here, and I hope you'll refer to this book time and again to refresh your memory. However, here are five key points that should stick with you long after you put the book down:

Know the Rules Before You Get in the Game: The overwhelming majority of business owners worldwide fail to develop the essential understanding of how businesses are effectively bought and sold in today's climate. The quality of your decisions will determine the quality of your exit. With the right knowledge, you can identify the right path—or roadmap—to be pursued which poses the highest probability of an extraordinary exit.

Exit Planning Is Critical: Selling your business requires advance planning. This can mean a few months up to two years of advance preparation. Understand the issues involved and set a realistic timeline of events so that you stay in control.

Creating a Competitive Bidding Scenario is Crucial: Without question, the surest way to ensure you receive the maximum price, best deal terms and highest probability of a successful transaction is through competitive bidders vying for your company.

The Importance of Sales and Marketing: Selling your business, despite what you may think or what others may tell you, is not fundamentally a matter of accounting. The numbers behind your business are imperative, yes, but it is primarily the effectiveness of the sales and marketing initiative that will generate the highest probability of a successful transaction.

Choose the Right Advisor: Selling a company has its ups and downs from beginning to end and can be emotionally, physically, and psychologically challenging. There will be challenges, surprises, disagreements, and tough questions to confront. Buyers may have a very different perspective regarding your projections, the outlook of your market, the robustness of your intellectual property, your client list, your senior management, and so on. The right advisor by your side, someone you like and trust and who anticipates and addresses these eventualities (and many more), is essential. That advisor must be able to build positive rapport with each investor, readily address the nuances of the process, negotiate effectively, and be someone you trust. They must possess the right experience and be committed to your sale process. That—all of that—will produce the highest probability of a successful result for you.

There is much to do. Let's begin.

CHAPTER 2

WHAT IS MY BUSINESS WORTH?

"Only a fool thinks price and value are the same."

—Antonio Machado

Of course, the thought has crossed your mind. It's often the first thing an owner wants to know. After all, most people don't feel they can even begin to think about selling until they have a sense of what the payoff will be.

"What is my business worth?" is a legitimate question that most accountants, and some consultants, will be happy to answer right away. You may hear some sort of rule of thumb like "6x–8x EBITDA is common in your industry," but always take such comments with the proverbial grain of salt. This is (a) potentially wrong in your case, and (b) immediately runs the risk of incorrectly setting your expectations either too low or too high.

The truth is that the answer to that question depends on many factors, some in your control, some not. Here's the important—very important—point to remember when you think about sale price:

**Your business will sell for exactly
what someone is prepared to pay for it**.

You can perceive the complexity embedded in this statement. What "someone is prepared to pay" depends enormously on the value you are delivering to them, and value varies hugely among buyers depending on their experiences, perspective, situation, the market, their strategy, their mind-set, what you have done with your company and what your company would do for them were they to acquire it. If you bring enough people to the table, through a process that entails speaking effectively to a pool of interested and qualified potential buyers, you'll quickly discover that what someone is prepared to pay can vary by **200%** or more between the lowest offer and the highest. The ultimate goal is for the price to reflect the full value of your business.

At the end of the day, valuation is not an exact process. Anyone who suggests otherwise has been reading too many academic books, rather than negotiating with buyers in the real world. A myriad of factors drive valuation of a given company, and different investors may ascribe different values to those factors. Different prospective investors will see different value based on the various synergies they identify in your company. For example, if one potential acquirer sees your geographic footprint and client base as the ideal solution for her expansion plans, she will value that component of your firm higher than another party who already operates in that territory.

So, price is subjective.

And while there's a degree of science involved in determining valuation, there's also an element of *subjectivity*—and that is that every buyer's circumstances, backgrounds, experiences and considerations are different, so for the same business—let's say *your business*, two buyers may propose two VERY different offers.

Consequently, it's a *subjective science*.

Remember: Valuation can be calculated. But price—the price that someone is prepared to pay you for your business—is negotiated. Your business is *really* only worth the price that someone is prepared to pay for it.

Another key contributor to the wide variation in value is rooted in the inefficiency of the market. To illustrate what I mean, let's compare selling a house to selling a business.

If you're selling a house, these points generally hold true:

- Buyers and sellers can find each other quickly and easily;
- There are many similar homes for sale nearby and there's plenty of recent transaction data;
- There's significant data available about your house, other houses, and the market;
- The market adjusts rapidly to new data such as interest rate changes;
- How you sell the house is unlikely to make a substantial difference in the price;
- Buyers are prequalified financially and you can close a deal quickly; and
- There is a large pool of buyers at any time.

These are all characteristics of an efficient market, and in an efficient market, asset prices generally fully reflect all the available information.

Now consider characteristics of the business market (especially for private companies not traded on a stock exchange):

- Information about similar transactions is not readily available— details about transactions of privately held companies generally remain private;
- Sellers and buyers cannot find each other easily;
- The process required to identify and engage with prospective buyers is measured in months;
- Determining the fit between buyer and seller is an engaging and time-consuming process;
- Negotiations and due diligence are involved and complex;
- Drafting definitive agreements can take a long time;

- The process you use to sell the business can have a significant impact on the price; and
- There is a limited pool of potential buyers worldwide.

These are characteristics of an inefficient, relatively opaque market. In a market such as this, prices will vary more widely than in an efficient market, so how you sell the business matters more. For example, if you are approached out of the blue by a potential buyer, it's much harder to know how their offer should be assessed. A pool of interested buyers will offer you a wide range of prices for your business, based on how they perceive its value, so how do you know where the suitor knocking on your door falls within that range? You don't, because you don't know who else is out there who also could be interested—potentially much more interested.

I have seen the effects of this opaque marketplace play out very badly. In one instance, I knew a seller who had started and built up a company that manufactured and supplied infrastructure materials to the telecommunications industry. She worked at it for a dozen years, achieving revenue and earnings growth every year but one. An American private equity (PE) firm approached her with an unsolicited bid to buy the company, and she accepted it, apparently motivated by the fact that the PE firm promised to close the deal quickly. Working with her existing lawyer and tax accountant, she went through the deal process without challenging any of the purchaser's conditions—no negotiations on price or deal terms, no effort to understand why the buyer was interested in the first place, nothing.

I heard about the deal after it had closed, and I was puzzled. She apparently hadn't negotiated effectively, and she hadn't done the work to understand the relative value of the deal on the table (we came to learn that her lawyers, a small practice located near her office, had no meaningful experience in M&A). Yet her company had a portfolio of intellectual property (patented or patent pending) and had recently brought to market an innovation that was poised to be a disruptive technology in her industry.

My team conducted a quick analysis of recent comparable transactions over the trailing 36 months and concluded that she had sold her company for roughly half of what it was worth. She had, quite literally, left a fortune on the table.

VALUATION METHODOLOGIES

As I mentioned before, valuation generally is more of an art than a science, though the analytical methods to assess valuation generally have rigorous academic theory behind them and can establish a realistic valuation range. The value of a company can be determined using several different methods.

Discounted Cash Flows: This calculation begins with free cash flow (FCF), roughly calculated this way:

(net income + interest expense + depreciation) - (capital expenditure + changes in working capital) = FCF

"Capital expenditure" is spending on long-term assets; "working capital" would be, for example, investments in inventory.

Once you've calculated free cash flow over time, a discount rate is applied. This rate is based on the risk of cash flows. Once the FCF has been projected for a period of time (usually around five years), a Terminal Value is calculated, usually as a *perpetuity* (for example, assuming that the company will operate in perpetuity with growth correlated with GDP growth, such as 2% to 3%) or as a multiple of the last year's EBITDA. Finally, a discount rate is applied to the projected cash flows that is intended to reduce the value of the future cash flows for two items: the time value of money (a dollar today is worth more than a dollar tomorrow) and risk (that projected dollar of EBITDA in the future may end up really being 50 cents).

	Year 1	Year 2	Year 3	Year 4	Year 5
EBITDA (earnings before interest, taxes, depreciation, and amortization)	$100	$110	$121	$133	$146
NOPAT: EBITDA x (1 - Tax Rate)	$60	$66	$73	$80	$88
Minus: Capital Expenditures	$10	$15	$15	$20	$15
Minus: Change in Working Capital	$12	$16	$18	$20	$22
Free Cash Flow (FCF) from Operations	$38	$35	$40	$40	$51
Terminal Value (e.g. 10X EBITDA)					$1,464
Present Value of FCF @ 20% Discount Rate	$32	$24	$23	$19	$609
NPV @ 20% Discount Rate	$707				

NOPAT=Net Operating Profit After Tax; NPV=Net Present Value, or "valuation" today; Tax Rate=40%

After these items have been calculated, you can discount the projected cash flow to determine the "valuation" today:

Multiples of EBITDA: Earnings before interest, taxes, depreciation, and amortization is a common way of clearing away the brush to show what a company actually earns. EBITDA allows an investor to determine the consequence of operating decisions while eliminating the impacts of non-operating decisions such as tax rates (a governmental decision), interest expenses (a financing decision) and large non-cash items, like depreciation and amortization (accounting decision). EBITDA enables investors to hone in on the operating profitability as a singular measure of performance. This is relevant when assessing similar companies across an industry, or when there is more than one company operating in different tax jurisdictions or tax brackets. Valuation parameters are then expressed as a multiple of EBITDA, and most industries have accepted benchmarks. Multiples are handy shortcuts to discounted cash flows, though the underlying logic is the same. Multiples reflect the analysis that the general market has performed, although as I already mentioned, the common EBITDA multiples in your industry may not be accurate for your firm for a number of reasons that are related to the specific details of your business.

Industry-Specific: Some industries have differing valuation parameters for reasons that are specific to that sector. The banking industry, for example, compares book value to market value, because they have different structures for reporting earnings. The mining industry considers mineral value to market value. Software companies often look at a multiple of revenue, rather than earnings. It's important to speak with your advisor to establish the right approach for your business and sector.

Recent transactions: Just as sales of homes in your neighborhood affect the valuation of your home, so do recent sales of other companies in your business, whether domestic or international. This data provides insight into the multiples the market is supporting at the moment as well as any relevant premiums or discounts being applied, compared to industry standards.

FINANCIAL BUYERS

A financial buyer is an investor interested in the return they can achieve by buying a business. They pursue the cash flow generated by that business and the future exit opportunities the business is likely to present.

Financial buyers are opportunistic buyers who may or may not have expertise in your industry. They often take on significant debt to finance a purchase, with an eye on short- to medium-term appreciation in the enterprise value of your business, or a broader consolidation play (buying and integrating companies in a particular sector to expand market power and gain economies of scale). They seek opportunities to invest in undervalued companies and/or companies poised for significant growth. During the period in which they hold the investment, they deliver the required financial support for growth, and plan to exit their investment for a profit in the short to medium term. Financial buyers typically are investment funds (private equity, venture capital, etc.) seeking to profit primarily by rearranging the operational and capital structure of your company—cutting costs, assuming increased debt, and leveraging their investment—with the view of selling in the future to realize a profit. The standard private equity hold period, for example, is typically five to seven years.[1]

A financial buyer's most sought-after targets typically possess reliable, established cash flows, high growth, low capital expenditure requirements, an established market position, and products or services in markets and industries that are growing. That said, different financial investors adapt different investment strategies. It is not uncommon to find financial investors with varied areas of focus, meaning that you will see groups of industry-specific funds (and often highly specialized, such as fintech,

---

1 Much is written in the press these days regarding private equity (PE). PE is an asset class that involves the use of securities and debt to purchase shares of private companies (or public companies that will subsequently delist). PE is a generic term used to identify a group of alternative investing methods, including buyout funds, growth equity funds, venture capital funds, special debt funds (mezzanine, distressed, etc.), certain real estate investment funds, and other types of special situations funds.

artificial intelligence and biotechnology funds), or turnaround specialists who purchase companies in distress, make major changes to the company, negotiate with creditors, and sell the company once stabilized.

Simply put, financial buyers purchase exactly what the company has to offer: the expected future earnings of the company at the time of the acquisition. They may acknowledge the potential for expanding cash flow beyond what the company has achieved on its own, but normally are not willing to pay for that potential. For most financial buyers, their intent is to grow the business and eventually sell to a strategic buyer or IPO the firm, if applicable.

One important differentiator between the two major classes of investors, financial buyers and strategic buyers, is frequently the financial buyer must be able to leverage the business—that is, borrow money for their investment and use operating profits to pay the interest. As you can imagine, the health and competitiveness of credit markets is a substantial factor in their calculations. The availability and cost of borrowed capital, among other considerations, can cap the price these investors will pay.[2]

Financial buyers typically are extremely sophisticated in terms of deal structure and diligence. They most often possess the internal expertise to carry out deep analysis, modeling the value of prospective purchases, deal structuring, and the legal expertise required to get the deal over the line. Given their focus on servicing debt as part of the deal, topics such as senior management quality, depth, and experience; sustainable EBITDA; and free cash flow are issues that the financial investor is more sensitive to.

Here are some of the advantages and disadvantages of selling to a financial buyer.

---

2 The private equity market has continued to grow robustly in recent years. The low-interest-rate environment that has characterized the global economy has fueled this growth, not only by making borrowed money relatively cheap, but also by driving investors to seek higher returns outside the debt markets. Fundraising and capital availability have reached record levels and global demand has significantly exceeded the supply of quality investment targets.

ADVANTAGES

- May provide access to deep pockets for future acquisitions and other growth initiatives
- Usually offers flexibility in determining most effective transaction structure
- Current management may be able to retain a meaningful degree of upside potential
- Current management and staff are likely to retain significant involvement in day-to-day direction and operation of the business
- May provide owner with ability to realize additional returns (earn-outs, etc.)
- May (if a successful PE fund) have advisors on retainer, with substantial industry expertise and networks
- Often causes less business disruption and negative impact on customer loyalty and employee morale

DISADVANTAGES

- Often requires ongoing involvement of owner in business going forward in short to medium term (which may also be an advantage to the owner, as this commitment could be associated with performance bonuses)
- Heavy debt service requirements may limit capital available to the company for growth
- Heavy debt load (and thus, associated interest costs) applied by the financial buyer diminishes the firm's margin for error
- Upside potential is reliant upon solid management direction and growth
- Financial buyers historically pay less than strategic buyers

- Typically requires robust financial reporting back to the financial investor

STRATEGIC BUYERS

Strategic buyers differ from financial buyers in that they are interested in how a company fits into and advances their own long-term business plans. They typically operate within a similar space as you and are seeking to acquire a company for more than just the cash flow. They seek to acquire companies that will add to the capabilities of their own company—or other companies—that they already own. Their reasons for acquiring your company may include:

- Entering into new geographic markets or product lines;
- Obtaining new customers or contracts;
- Eliminating a competitor; or
- Acquiring new skills or capabilities such as:
  - Distribution,
  - R&D capacity, or
  - Intellectual property.

Consequently, a strategic buyer is often prepared—and able—to pay a higher price than a financial buyer.

The strategic buyer sees the target—your company—as a way to acquire those elements that fit with or enhance their existing business. This decision is often motivated by the rationale that it is cheaper and faster to acquire an existing company than it is to build or develop their own from scratch. This growth-by-acquisition is a common cornerstone of many growth strategies.

SOURCES OF STRATEGIC BUYERS

Most strategic buyers come from one of the following:

SUPPLIER INDUSTRIES

Suppliers typically look for an acquisition of their customer to produce vertical integration (combining elements of the supply chain). By combining two parts of the supply chain, an acquirer may be in a position to capture higher margins and access a more attractive customer base.

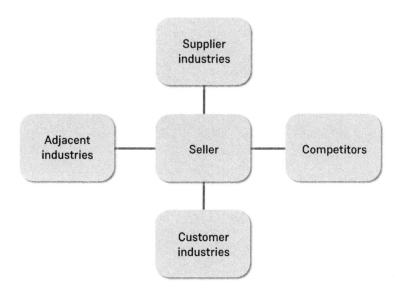

CUSTOMER INDUSTRIES

Customers may wish to acquire your business for similar reasons to suppliers, particularly if you sell to only a few customers.

COMPETITORS

Competitors may seek to acquire your business to consolidate their position in the market and to gain leverage in negotiations with suppliers and customers.

ADJACENT INDUSTRIES

"Adjacencies" refer to businesses that are either in the same industry in a different geography, or the same geography selling a product close to yours. For example, adjacencies for CVS Pharmacy in the US could include Boots (pharmacy chain in the UK), and Whole Foods (a US grocery chain selling to similar customers as CVS).

As a business gets larger, the market of potential buyers grows—up to a point. For a typical business deal of $250 million or less (those normally handled by an M&A advisor), my firm, for example, will construct a plan of whom to contact and what countries to target. We typically end up with a fairly large list of potential targets, with strategic buyers on average representing 85 percent of the list and financial buyers making up the other 15 percent. Depending on the nature of our client's business, we expect to compile a list of 100–400 potential buyers. Many of these candidate buyers are not actively looking to make a purchase, but often will respond favorably to a solid opportunity presented to them the right way.

STRATEGICS PAY FOR SYNERGY

Several studies of completed sales have found that strategic buyers pay more than financial buyers. Specifically, the median private equity financial buyer paid 9.5x EBITDA, while the median strategic buyer paid 10.4x EBITDA (9.4% higher). The average (mean) multiple was even higher: private equity firms paid 17.8x EBITDA, while strategic buyers paid 21.3x (a premium of 19.6%). And the most expensive 5% of deals had an even greater disparity, with private equity paying an average of 51.2x EBITDA and strategics 72.5x EBITDA.[3]

Of course, no rule is hard and fast, but there are two consistent reasons strategics generally are willing to pay more. The primary reason: synergy. Synergy is the additional value that is generated by combining two firms, creating opportunities that would not have been available to these firms operating independently. Synergy gains arising from operational improvements are often used by acquirers to justify mergers—and the greater the value of the perceived synergies, the greater the interest in your company— and the greater the price, usually. In short, the better the fit (i.e., the more realizable the synergies are), the more they will desire the business and the greater the premium they will pay.

Synergy is the most widely used, and sometimes misused, term in mergers and acquisitions. Because this is such a key concept, I'm going to dive into it a bit here. As I mentioned above, synergy is the idea of 2+2=5: the value and performance of two companies combined will be greater than the sum of the separate individual parts. It can also be defined as the potential financial benefit achieved through combining the companies. Many strategic investors will invest a great deal of time identifying the synergies associated with your firm. From the strategic investor executive team's perspective, their shareholders will benefit if their post-merger company value increases due to the synergistic effect of the deal.

TYPICAL AREAS OF SYNERGY INCLUDE:

- Increase customer base
- Access to new markets

---

3 Massachusetts Institute of Technology study on strategic and financial bidders in competitive sales process in 349 U.S. deals between 2000 and 2008; Copenhagen Business School: Western European acquisitions from 1997–2013, a study of 1,332 transactions including 418 consummated with a financial buyer and 914 with a strategic buyer; Rotterdam School of Management study on 410 transactions: 205 private equity deals within the United States from 1997–2006; St. Gallen University, "Do Private Equity Funds Always Pay Less?" S. Morkotter/T. Welzer, Oct 2016.

- Geographic diversification
- Access to new brands
- Higher growth potential
- Taking a competitor out of the market
- Increased market share
- Increased talent
- Intellectual property/proprietary know-how
- Expanded geographical footprint
- Improved reputation
- Increased economies of scale
  (such as increased leverage with suppliers and customers)
- Reduced operating expense
- Increased pricing power
- Access to distribution channels
- Increased revenue

You can see that some of these synergies offer more immediate benefits (increased market share, reduced operating costs), and some offer longer-term benefits, such as higher growth potential. When synergies are substantial, it's not surprising that a buyer may be willing to pay substantially more for your business—particularly if those synergies are unique to that buyer. A good advisor will be able to sniff these situations out and capitalize on them.

One factor to consider with a strategic buyer is the consequences to your employees and other stakeholders. For example, to realize expected synergies, a buyer may plan to eliminate much of your management team or staff. Every buyer has a different plan, but if the implications of a sale to your team are a matter of critical importance to you, it's best to discuss those post-sale plans with a potential buyer.

The second reason strategic buyers may pay more for your business is that they generally are larger companies with better access to inexpensive capital. And they often have another currency available to them: stock. Strategic buyers often offer stock, cash, or a combination of the two in payment of the purchase price. They have more purchasing tools to work with than most financial buyers.

In short, the strategic buyer buys your company to enhance existing operations. Rather than simply paying for cash flow, they are willing to pay for two other things: readily achievable synergies, such as increased efficiency, and theoretical synergies, such as greater opportunity to grow. This is particularly true if your potential buyer is a competitor approached through a competitive bidding process (more on this later). And that strategic buyer likely has more tools to get the deal done.

Here are some of the advantages and disadvantages of selling to a strategic buyer.

ADVANTAGES

- May provide highest valuation for shareholders in the near term
- May enable the entrepreneur the opportunity to completely walk away (obtain the greatest liquidity)
- May provide attractive career opportunities for the management team
- Potential operating synergies can improve the business
- No immediate plans to "flip" or sell the company

DISADVANTAGES

- Some management may lose their jobs, their autonomy, or have their roles diminished

- Possible negative impact on culture and morale
- May affect customer loyalty
- Upside value potential for the seller may be sacrificed (unless there is significant stock or earn-out consideration)
- The risk of being trapped in bureaucratic delay, i.e., decision paralysis on the buyer's part is more significant than with a financial buyer

THE VALUE OF YOUR COMPANY

An important concept to consider regarding potential buyers is "the best owner principle."[4] Simply stated, this means that a business's value varies under different (or potential) owners. Each party's value is based on how they manage it, what strategy they employ and how well they can execute such a strategy. In this context, the "best owner" is not necessarily the person who is going to look after your management team or keep running the business the way you would have done. The best owner is the person who can justify the highest price because they are in a position to extract the most value. That generally comes down to the synergies identified between the buyer's and seller's businesses.

For example, imagine that your company develops enterprise software for large organizations. One potential buyer makes and distributes software for small businesses and another makes and distributes analytical tools for large organizations. Between the two, the second buyer is likely to be the best owner; they can extract more value from your company because what you do is a better fit with what they do (i.e., they can leverage each other's similar customers to cross-sell products).

---

4 *McKinsey Quarterly*, November 2009, "Are You Still the Best Owner of Your Assets?"

Of course, there is certainly a time and place in the sales process for weighing other considerations (such as how a new buyer plans to treat your existing team), but that is not in the best owner calculation.

***

I like to think of valuation as an iterative process that is influenced by a number of factors. Some of these, such as your bottom line, you can control to a greater or lesser degree. Some of them, such as business cycles, the synergies a particular buyer desires, and the larger economy, you cannot. And as a buyer goes through pre-LOI (Letter of Intent) due diligence, what they learn will influence how they value your company. In other words, the results of pre-LOI due diligence shape the valuation of the company. Consequently, as a seller you should be prepared for the valuation number to evolve throughout the pre-LOI due diligence process. Your—and your advisor's—job is to build strong, credible messages around the quality of earnings, the synergies between your firm and the potential buyer, and develop a dynamic due diligence process that prepares your team to respond positively to buyer analysis, potential skepticism, and rigorous negotiations.

Your M&A advisor will help you establish the valuation parameters for your company. They should be able to demonstrate that their calculations are a supported opinion, not simply a price they have inflated to excite you and to secure your business. Sellers can be in for a rude awakening if they haven't been appropriately counselled by their advisor, and then discover down the line that buyers have a very different sense of a company's value. An M&A advisor is responsible for bridging gaps, but if the gap is a result of wildly optimistic estimates, then they may not be able to do so.

Sometimes the value of your company depends, in part, on luck. We worked with a software company that developed products around managing and maintaining heavy equipment—the complicated machines used in mining, oil and gas production, big industrial installations, and so on. The buyer's business was founded by engineers who had built an industrial support services organization. They looked at the landscape and realized that they needed to pivot toward being a technology organization. They knew they had to change. Rather than try to reinvent themselves from the inside out, they chose to buy our client's business, a company that already had the expertise and intellectual property that they needed. These engineers were prepared to pay a premium for a turnkey solution for their strategic problem.

You can't plan on a lucky break like that. On the other hand, luck is what happens when preparation meets opportunity. One client had spent a fortune developing his own supercar company. Unlike so many of his predecessors who set out to develop a supercar only to create something that looked "homemade" or worse, this guy built a truly phenomenal car—two, in fact.

Once the world's leading automotive press had confirmed the breathtaking performance, engineering, and styling of the vehicles, he promptly shut the operation down. His goal had not been to develop a successful car company but to prove to himself that he could produce his own car that would rival the world's best. And he did. Resoundingly. Now he wanted to get rid of it. But what is something like that worth?

We had the mandate to sell the intellectual property (designs, software developments, etc.) and a small inventory of parts sufficient to manufacture six to eight more vehicles—essentially a warehouse full of engines, carbon fiber bodies, and all the bits and pieces required to build a small fleet of supercars.

One of our potential buyers was a charismatic Middle Eastern businessman who was a car collector and avid racing fan. He made a low offer, explaining that there was no brand behind the car and that he would have to invest in establishing a brand of his own. We responded by advising that if we would not value the brand, we would retain the brand name and he could simply purchase the other assets, namely the components, designs, and software. "But I need the brand name," he countered, "as that's the name that everyone can Google to see all the favorable press the cars have received." He had directly contradicted his own argument that the brand itself was worthless. We sat back down and negotiated a revised figure that ascribed a fairer value to the brand.

The point here is that valuation is as much an art as it is a science. I don't believe that this gentleman was trying to pick up the brand at no cost; rather, he had not fully appreciated the value the brand brought him. Once we engaged in an open discussion on the issue, he quickly came to see that the brand name was, in fact, an important element to the overall sale. When you are negotiating, you need to be in control of the discussion. Make sure your advisor is capable and experienced in controlling negotiations and that they will not hesitate for a moment to push back on any aspects of the valuation discussion that are of a disadvantage to you and your other shareholders.

Value can also come down to timing, particularly around business or market cycles. Recently we sold a business that's involved in creating and running co-working office spaces. This is a fast-growing business, and investors are clamoring to get into it. We secured a very attractive deal for our client. The original owners retained a minority equity position; experienced an attractive return on their investment; have a globally recognized investor backing them; much more capital to grow the business with; and are now facing the very real prospect of considerable upside return as the company grows.

Timing can work against you, of course. We worked with a company in the logistics space that had an innovative approach to shipping parcels. They got a good offer but decided not to sell at the time. Two years later their suppliers were squeezing them hard, and their competitors had effectively caught up with them (a few had surpassed them). For various personal reasons, they had to sell or would likely face the eventual threat of bankruptcy. They received—and took—a much less attractive offer.

* * *

Remember that rule of thumb example of "6x-8x EBITDA"? You can see why it is simplistic to the point of being nonsensical, and potentially harmful as you begin to navigate the process of valuing your business and positioning it for an optimal sale. I'll spare you the long explanation of how accounting methods can skew calculation of EBITDA and multiples to make them even less reliable as true measures of business value.

What matters is not rules of thumb, but understanding buyer motivations. Motives, not multiples of EBITDA, are what propel valuations. Recognize the motivations of the buyer and you begin to appreciate the approach they will implement in valuing the business. Motivations can influence value or multiples of profit. Should they offer what seems like a low bid based on their perspective (financial or strategic), an informed and properly advised seller will recognize that there is almost always a higher figure in the acquirer's mind. This point alone can prove to be the difference between a good offer and a great one.

To find that small group of qualified and interested investors with powerful motives to purchase your business you are going to have to identify, research, and engage with a large number of potential investors. In other words, you're going to have to kiss a lot of frogs. So how do those frogs view you?

VALUE DRIVERS

Ask yourself this simple question: *Could I sell my business today?*

It's a straightforward query, but one that very few business owners regularly ask themselves. Would you be in the position to respond to a purchaser today if they were to make an unsolicited bid to acquire your business?

For most entrepreneurs, the answer is a clear "no." I expect as soon as you asked yourself that question, a flood of reasons you couldn't sell today came to mind. Just as you have to hire a yard maintenance crew and a painter before you put your house on the market, you want to get your business in order before you proceed. First impressions count—and not only toward establishing credibility that your business is a valuable acquisition target. Impressions also contribute toward a favorable valuation. Understanding that, you now know where to begin.

Value drivers are the real, as well as perceived, features of a company that improve the company's value from the perspective of the investor. It's important that you and your M&A advisor recognize and understand these drivers. By knowing your value strengths and weakness early in the sales process, you have time and opportunity to shore up your offering and elicit the highest price. If you've ever sold a house, you are familiar with this experience. The process I'm describing here is in some ways equivalent to refinishing the floors, adding a fresh coat of paint, trimming the shrubbery, and repairing that leaky faucet in the bathroom before buyers begin walking through your home. However, it goes beyond that—think, "remodeling the kitchen" and "adding an in-ground pool." Improving your value drivers means making changes to the business that make the company more resilient on its own and improve the value of the company in the mind of a strategic buyer.

CHARACTERISTIC VALUE DRIVERS INCLUDE:

- The combination of resources and capabilities that allow you to generate a sustainable competitive advantage;
- The long-term viability of your market(s);
- Reputation of your business;
- People and intellectual capital—overall quality and experience of the management team;
- Customer list and relationships with those parties;
- Track record of financial success, cash flow, and profitability;
- Intellectual property, such as technology/software, patents, trademarks, and brand name;
- Growth trends/projections for key (or new/innovative) products and services; and
- Synergies expected by the acquirer from a merger/acquisition.

Once you've identified your value drivers you can begin to evaluate the strength of each and, where appropriate, implement a plan to improve them. For example, your IT systems may be outdated and not scalable to support the aggressive growth plans that a new owner may have in mind. You may determine that an upgrade is in order. You may decide that the business would be best served by allocating elements of your back office or manufacturing to offshore solutions. Similarly, your balance sheet and cash flow may require improvement, perhaps through cost cutting or debt restructuring. Or maybe it's time to restructure or retrain your management team. A clear-eyed assessment of your strengths and weaknesses from a potential buyer's perspective is essential.

***

Put yourself in the shoes of the investor. They are seeking to understand whether this company, *your* company, will continue to perform—and grow—in a post-acquisition setting. Your ability to provide this reassurance is based on an assortment of factors.

For example:

- Would you be able to present a potential buyer with a business plan that articulates your growth strategy?
- Does the plan address short- and medium-term issues to preserve value through a potential transition to new ownership?
- As the leader of the firm, how essential is your day-to-day presence in the operations of the company—in other words, if you left, would it struggle in your absence? If the current management is not capable of filling your shoes after you've departed, the investor will have less assurance about a potential acquisition or will require you to remain with the company for a number of years after the sale.

These are questions that investors will be asking themselves—and you—about your firm.

If you were the investor acquiring this business, what concerns would you have when you looked at your company for the first time? This is not an easy exercise—it requires you to be dispassionate and critical of the very thing you have poured your heart and soul into. Check your ego at the door and walk through your company in a buyer's wingtips (or pumps, or Nikes).

This is not the time for you to proudly defend the various characteristics of your company. Instead, look for problems. Undertake a complete, unblinking assessment of your company in an unbiased manner, looking for the areas within the business that may not live up to an investor's expectations or requirements. This is a tougher exercise to conduct than it may first appear. The company is your baby and you're now being asked to find every wart and wrinkle.

Here are some of the major areas you should examine with a buyer's eye.

BUSINESS AND FINANCIAL MATTERS

Developing an annual business plan makes good sense in any event. Having one to present to an investor will assure him or her that you have considered the factors affecting your company and have a robust strategy in place. It should include:

- Your company's growth strategy
- Who your competitors are and how your products or services are positioned
- Macro and micro trends related to your industry
- Three-year financial projections that are realistic and defendable
- SWOT (Strengths, Weaknesses, Opportunities and Threats) analysis

Demonstrating that you know your competitors, the trends arising in your sector, and how your products and services can best be positioned to succeed in an ever-changing marketplace will add to a buyer's overall confidence in your company.

Many external advisors—M&A advisors and others—can guide you through this exercise or conduct the exercise on your behalf in consultation with you. This process takes some time, as any external party needs first to develop an in-depth understanding of your business and sector, historical performance, customer base, sales and marketing strategy, financial performance and so on, before they can begin to draft a realistic and credible business plan.

FINANCIALS

Investors considering the acquisition of a company make key decisions based on the financial condition of a business. Naturally, they require consistent and reliable information from the seller. Anyone seriously considering acquiring your company is entitled to scrutinize financial statements, as well as your company's books and records. The last thing you want is for your statements to raise doubts in the buyer's mind. To prevent this, commission an audit or vendor due diligence report.

Any questions related to the reliability of your financial statements virtually disappear when a qualified public accounting firm has audited them. Unless your company is small (in which case a vendor due diligence report may be more appropriate), investors require financials that have been externally audited, generally by a well-known, appropriately credentialed firm. Unaudited accounts, or accounts that do not follow a standard framework of guidelines such as Generally Accepted Accounting Principles (GAAP) or International Financial Reporting Standards (IFRS), can be a costly and even deal-breaking mistake.

THE EXTERNAL AUDIT

An audit of your accounts by a credible and well-known firm, such as one of the "Big Four" (PwC, Deloitte, Ernst & Young, or KPMG), is not an inexpensive exercise. But it will give the buyer added confidence in the integrity of your financial statements. If the price tag for a Big Four audit is too hefty, consider a Top 20 firm or leading regional firm. Don't be afraid to speak with several firms to find the best fit and price for you. A quick Google search of "top 20 accounting firms" or similar will produce an immediate list for you to use as a starting point.

Here's how the process works, and some key things to pay attention to.

To begin, you select an external auditor. Don't hire a firm based solely on its name; instead, assess a short list of appropriate auditors and select the party that not only has the qualifications, but also has the experience in your industry.

Your auditor will plan out a schedule of work and initiate a diligent process of observation, inquiry, and inspection of internal financial books and records. Auditors will come to your offices and work closely with your team, who will need to be entirely forthcoming with them. Auditors will carry out various tests, such as requesting confirmations of orders from a sampling of customers, to prove the accuracy of items in the financial statements.

During the process, which may take as little as a few weeks or as long as a few months, depending on the scope and complexity of the work, the auditors will construct an audit trail—a chronological record of transactions—that enables them to evaluate internal controls, financial system designs and company policies. Auditors do not look at every transaction; rather, they evaluate a representative sample that will allow them to write their report with a high degree of confidence.

When the audit team has completed its work, it will prepare the Auditor's Report, containing the auditors' findings about the financial statements and to what extent they conform to generally accepted accounting principles (GAAP).

Commissioning an audit is a step you can initiate early in the process of preparing your business for sale.

NORMALIZING EBITDA

We discussed EBITDA earlier, but I am expanding upon it here to ensure that you are familiar with its definition and use in M&A transactions. As I explained, EBITDA, or earnings before interest, tax, depreciation, and amortization, is commonly used as a consistent, clear measure of how to value a business (for most industries). EBITDA is a number that eliminates sometimes ambiguous or inconsistent expenses. It is a widely used, apples-to-apples indicator that can be used across an industry to assess one firm's performance against another.

By eliminating interest, tax, depreciation, and amortization, EBITDA makes it easier to compare the underlying financial health of various companies. Why exclude these costs, which can be very real? They can indeed, but they also reflect management decisions that a buyer may or may not decide to change.

Interest is mainly a function of management's choices about capital structure. The level of debt a company uses has a direct impact on net income. How a company chooses to finance itself should not affect its inherent value. Interest can distort free cash flow if not removed.

Taxes are excluded because they are dependent on multiple variables, including the tax jurisdiction where the company is domiciled and carry-forward losses from previous years. These variations can distort net income, and so are excluded.

Depreciation and Amortization are non-cash expenses that can be subjective and arbitrary. They are based on specific accounting regulations that can be very different depending on the asset and where in the world the company operates. Accordingly, they are excluded from operating results for valuation purposes.

THE NORMALIZATION PROCESS

After your accountant arrives at EBITDA, you still do not have a good apples-to-apples number for a potential buyer to evaluate. The next step is "normalizing" EBITDA. This means adding back any extraordinary expenses such as discretionary, non-recurring, and owner-related expenses that the new owner would not expect to incur once he acquires the business. These add-backs depict a clearer understanding of the underlying earnings capacity of the business for the new owner once the deal is concluded. The resulting normalized EBITDA figure represents the future earnings capacity that a buyer could realistically expect from the business.

Given the subjective nature of the normalization process (making the case for which expenses should be added back to EBITDA can give rise to disputes between seller and buyer), you can see how there is potential disagreement and subsequent debate here. Because price offered is commonly based on a multiple of normalized EBITDA, buyers will maintain that sellers and their advisors have an incentive to take liberties and "normalize up" a company's EBITDA when marketing a business.

However, buyers are usually sophisticated and well advised themselves, and will be on the lookout for normalization adjustments that add money to the bottom line that don't seem justified. Expect a significant share of buyer due diligence to be dedicated to reviewing normalization adjustments. Buyers will also look to deduct non-recurring income items from EBITDA, such as sale of an asset, which has been used to boost EBITDA, but isn't consistent from year to year (and thus cannot be relied upon each year).

Common items requiring a normalization adjustment to EBITDA include:

- Owner and management salaries (to the extent they are different from the market). Consideration is generally given to what a normal range of management salaries would be for the new owners to operate the company effectively. Current owners may be overpaying or underpaying themselves.
- Family members or others on the books, who may not be performing a typical or even full-time job, but who draw a salary or receive other benefits.
- Costs incurred by owners that would not exist under new ownership. These can include automobiles, mobile/cell phones, gas cards, car insurance, travel, home office costs, and other owner perks.
- Perks that will not exist under new ownership. For example, generous bonuses, excessive travel stipends, personal meals, entertainment, and memberships.
- Legal/litigation items. Should your business be undergoing any one-time or highly unusual lawsuits, it would be appropriate to add these costs back.
- Repairs and maintenance. Often ignored, repairs and maintenance expenses can have a meaningful impact on EBITDA. Private business owners will often categorize capital expenses as repairs in order to minimize taxes. While this practice may reduce tax burden, it will adversely affect the valuation as it reduces historical EBITDA. Consequently, an appropriate review to separate and add any of these capital items back to EBITDA is an important exercise. These costs do not go away, but would be capitalized and expensed over time.
- Commercial rent or property costs. Normally these are adjusted to reflect actual market costs that would be incurred if the

business premises were to be leased by the new owner at current market rates.

As you might expect, buyers and sellers both pay a lot of attention to normalizing EBITDA, and this can cut both ways. In 2015, I had a client who manufactured lighting supplies. He set a very realistic goal of selling his company for 6x EBITDA. This, he thought, would fulfill his financial goals. My team was confident he would experience a multiple much higher, as we already had received indications of serious interest from two parties who valued the firm in the range of 9x–11x—and this was before we had even commenced our outreach to create a competitive bidding scenario for his company.

This owner had not considered normalizing EBITDA—it simply was a topic he had not discussed with his accountant. During our EBITDA adjustment analysis, we identified $312,000 in adjustments to be added back, increasing his earnings. These adjustments, all of which were straightforward and clearly justifiable, would—at a 6x valuation—bring the owners an additional $1.87 million. If the company sold at the high end of 11x, that windfall would be $3.43 million. Since he and his wife owned 100% of the shares, this was good news indeed.

During negotiations with the ultimate buyer, we made two concessions to bring the add-back down to $287,000 in the spirit of keeping the deal moving. But the final sales price was 12.8x EBITDA. That normalizing exercise had yielded almost $3.67 million in additional consideration paid by the buyer.

In another instance, my team was reviewing a seller's financial statement on behalf of a client who was in negotiations to purchase a home improvement business. Almost every account had an adjustment and we were having a hard time taking it all in. Why, for example, was there an add-back adjustment of $16,500 for tools and equipment? The seller's advisor told me it was a one-time expense, and the tools purchased last a long time. "Okay," I said, "then why was there a similar adjustment the year prior?" "Different tools," the advisor said. The evidence suggested that operating this business meant regularly purchasing tools, but the seller was trying to convince us that wasn't the case. If he could, he would be able to add back tens of thousands of dollars of allegedly "one-time" expenses as an EBITDA adjustment. (He did not, by the way, convince us.)

WHY SHOULD I SELL—AND WHEN?

So you've begun to get a sense of what your business is worth. Now what? Perhaps you've found yourself thinking lately about life after work. You like the sound of longer vacations, traveling the world, building your own boat, embarking upon another commercial pursuit, or simply spending more time with family. Or perhaps a potential buyer approached you and mentioned a price high enough to be intriguing. Whatever the reason, something inside of you has been telling you that it may be time to sell.

Owners sell for a multitude of reasons. The list is long, but the most common include:

- The retirement of the primary shareholder, who is often the founder
- To pursue a new commercial challenge
- Lack of expertise or desire to take the business to the next level
- To spend more time with family, grandchildren, or friends
- To travel the world
- The desire for liquidity and asset diversification on the part of the primary shareholder
- Competitive pressures

- Burnout
- Financial difficulties
- Death or illness of the owner
- The readiness of the next generation to take control of the business
- Loss of passion to drive the business
- Divorce

No matter what your reason is, you'll wonder about the timing. When should you sell?

The answer is: It depends.

The issues related to your business—and your own life, for that matter—are different from those of any other business or individual. Only you can clearly define your objectives and priorities. Only you can fully consider the circumstances of your life and your company and answer the most important questions. These answers will, in turn, lead you to an understanding of when you should sell—or if you should sell at all.

Here are some questions to jump-start that process of introspection and consideration.

- Should the business remain within the family—and why? Do any family members want the business? Would an ownership transition within the family create conflicts or otherwise negatively affect the family itself?
- What is most important to me? Price received? A good home for my business? Protection of staff? My continued involvement in the business post-transaction? The long-term performance or profile of the business?
- If I sell, do I want, or would I accept, a continuing management role in the business and if so, for how long after the sale would I be prepared to do so?

- Can the business stand without me yet? If I left today, is the management talent required to continue forward already in place? Is the business overly reliant upon me or other key stakeholders that may depart the business after it is sold?

- Are there any employees or other individuals that I specifically want to reward when the business is sold? Is there pressure or expectation on me to do that?

- Do I have a preference about the type of buyer—competitors, strategic investors, financial investors, and so on? Does it *really* matter to me?

- Do I want to keep an equity stake in the business? Am I prepared to accept an earn-out as part of the total consideration paid for my business? Does it need to be an all-cash transaction? Would I accept shares in the acquirer's company as part of the price paid for my business?

- Could my business grow faster or be more resilient if it was part of a larger company?

- What are my financial requirements for the short, medium, and long term?

Identifying and answering these questions long before you embark upon the journey to sell your business will provide direction and clarity, guiding you through the many decisions necessary on the path ahead. Whatever decision you take, it's only via a clear understanding of your personal, family, and business priorities that you will be able to select the exit options that will best meet your needs. This understanding is the bedrock of a successful sale of your business.

These questions are the tip of the iceberg. Break your considerations down into manageable pieces. The way to eat an elephant, after all, is one bite at a time. And once you do have a clear picture of where you want to go, bear in mind that there are factors beyond your control. The state of the market in your industry, for example, can make a huge difference in the valuation of your business and how attractive it is to potential buyers. Remember the examples above of the logistics company that was overwhelmed by competitive pressures, versus the co-working company that was riding a growing wave of interest. Different market situations lead to different outcomes.

SHOULD I LIST A VALUE?

After you've gone through the work of valuing your business, you and your deal team may be inclined to include that as part of the process of listing your business for sale. Many advisors suggest you do this, but my partners and I could not disagree more. If your strategy is to cast a wide net, engaging a multitude of domestic and international strategic and financial buyers with the objective of creating a competitive bidding process, the market will ultimately respond with how much value they attribute to your business. If you publish a price, guess the maximum price you are likely to receive? On the other hand, it *can* be helpful to publish a minimum required bid so potential buyers will know if they're in the ballpark. By letting the market respond and then negotiating with each interested party to maximize the price each is willing to pay is the surest way to elicit the highest price. Remember, your business is worth exactly what someone is willing to pay for it. So don't tell them what they'll pay—ask them.

While there are aspects to selling your business you cannot control, there is a great deal that you can. Begin with the end in mind. Get clear in your head about why you want to sell, what matters to you, and how you are going to achieve it. Educate yourself about the process by consulting the right people in the right order. Proceed methodically, and with the right team and the right plan, you have the best chance of navigating to a successful sale.

In 2010, when the effects of the recession were still being felt, we were approached by an Icelandic bank to help sell a golf resort they had repossessed. The place was gorgeous, complete with a 27-hole golf course, 200 finished, never-inhabited homes, a five-star spa, and more. Yet in nearly two years of trying, employing three different advisors, each of whom employed a passive approach of listing the property for sale but not actively selling, they had elicited only one single offer (which was so low, it was immediately dismissed). They had no strategy, they had too much on their plate, and they couldn't effectively navigate the market. Within eight weeks we had fourteen solid offers on the table for them, and they ended up selling for three percent more than their "magic wand" price stated at the outset. In many ways they were lucky, because by failing to close a sale before, they had avoided making a bad deal. Trying to learn by doing, they did pay a high cost carrying that property for two years. But they avoided the most pernicious outcome, which is closing a subpar deal. In situations like that, you never really know how much money you left behind.

What Is My Business Worth?

The Intelligent Exit

CHAPTER 3

EXIT PLANNING

> *"Before anything else, preparation is the key to success."*
>
> —Alexander Graham Bell

If you want to sabotage the sale of your business, skip this chapter.

Despite overwhelming evidence that exit planning is a vital component of successful business ownership, most business owners don't do the work to create a plan. And lack of planning on the seller's part is the number one reason that private business sales fail or only partially succeed.[5]

You may have seen Stephen Covey's simple time management matrix, sometimes called the "Urgent vs. Important Matrix." *Urgent* is on the X axis, *Important* on the Y axis. There are four resulting quadrants: *Urgent & Important, Urgent & Not Important, Not Urgent & Not Important, and Not Urgent & Important.* Most of us spend our time living in the first three. We know we should spend time on the things that are in the last quadrant, *Not Urgent & Important,* but it's hard to do so. As an owner, you likely are busy running the company day to day, putting out fires. Finding the time to delve into the issues that comprise an exit strategy is the sort of thing that keeps getting pushed back. And so that's where your exit plan lives, in the land of *Not Urgent & Important.*

---

5 Pricewaterhouse Coopers, "Whose Business Is It Anyway: Smart Strategies for Ownership Succession"

	URGENT	NOT URGENT
IMPORTANT	**Quadrant I** *Urgent* *&* *Important*	**Quadrant II** *Not Urgent* *&* *Important*
NOT IMPORTANT	**Quadrant III** *Urgent* *&* *Not Important*	**Quadrant IV** *Not Urgent* *&* *Not Important*

Until it is urgent. Then you may be in a bind. A well-constructed exit plan is a tool that equips you to get the best deal you can, in every way. But it isn't something you can create overnight, which is why you should start working on one now.

THE PURPOSE OF THE EXIT PLAN

What do you want? And how are you going to achieve it? An exit plan answers those questions—and more. It is a strategic guide serving as your road map, allowing you to successfully transition to the next phase of your life after you've sold your company—which, after all, should be the ultimate goal of any sale.

Perhaps you want your children to carry on your company. Or you want an investor who will bring in the resources to enable you to take your company to the next level. Or you're ready to cash out and sail away. Whatever your goal, understand it first.

Honestly, you cannot start too soon. Depending on the specifics of your business, effective exit planning can take months—for some, even years before you have all the pieces in place (for instance, how long would it take for you, as the business owner, to make yourself redundant in day-to-day operations so that you can depart the business once sold?). One goal of this planning is to remain in control, rather than be dictated to by events. A good plan provides you with readiness and agility if an opportunity presents itself. And good planning is likely to give you leverage with a potential buyer. You'll be confident in your strengths; you'll be fully prepared. You'll have a solid grip on the value you can deliver and the synergies you can create.

CAVEAT EMPTOR

Much has been written on the issue of exit planning. Most of it is accurate and has merit, while some of it is entirely self-serving and, to a lesser extent, just bad advice. Most investment bankers, advisors, brokers, lawyers, and accountants will be quite free with their suggestions that you pursue one particular course of action or another. You might notice, however, that their recommendations seem to line up with the specific services they offer, so caveat emptor.

An exit plan accomplishes several things at once:

- Ensures the readiness of your firm to be acquired by an investor;
- Ensures that YOU are prepared in all respects, both commercially and emotionally/psychologically for the exit process ahead;
- Maximizes the value of the business at the time of exit;
- Minimizes stress on you, your staff, and the new owner;
- Maximizes tax incentives available to you; and, most importantly;

- Safeguards your personal and financial goals.

Although exit plans can vary from owner to owner, a typical complete exit planning strategy addresses the following fundamental components:

- Your goals and objectives
- All information prepared and ready in advance
- Business valuation parameters established
- Value driver analysis
- Value enhancement opportunities
- Exit options analysis
- Strategic timing
- Tax and net proceeds calculation
- Recommendations

By identifying this information, you and your co-shareholders can make decisions on an informed basis. You will be able to:

- Maintain greater control over how and when you exit;
- Minimize the emotional stress of the exit process;
- Maximize your company's value in good times and bad;
- Minimize or defer capital gains taxes;
- Select the best exit options and the best timing;
- Ensure you achieve all of your business and personal goals; and
- Minimize your stress as well as the stress on your employees and families.

Conversely, the failure to develop an exit strategy can set the stage for the following potential outcomes:

- Relinquishing a degree of control over the process by being reactive rather than proactive;
- Undervaluing your company and leaving hard-earned wealth on the table;
- Paying too much in taxes;
- Being forced to sell your company as a result of an unforeseen event (likely one of the four Ds: death, disability, divorce, or distress);
- Failing to realize all of your business and personal goals; and
- Inflicting unnecessary stress or anxiety on your family, your employees, and yourself.

In my experience, most owners find that when they finally do embark upon the exit planning process it's not as time-consuming as they feared. Often, they discover that they already know a lot about many of the areas the plan addresses. They also develop a sense of enthusiasm and motivation to drive the process to its conclusion, energized by the fact that they have a greater sense of focus and strategy that will lead them to achieving their goals.

With sufficient lead time, you and your advisor will accomplish the following as part of exit planning. These are the bedrock on which all your other work will rest:

- Create monthly or quarterly reports that allow a future buyer to understand key performance metrics.
- Demonstrate that you have long-term relationships with customers and vendors.
- Ensure that an effective management team is in place.
- Accurately recognize the strengths and weaknesses of your business, and take actions to adjust.
- Ensure that senior management have updated employment contracts in place.

- Resolve any outstanding litigation or other legal matters (where possible).
- Alter your strategic plan to create a more attractive asset for sale.
- Put your financial house in order.
- Develop a clear and convincing message around quality of earnings and performance.
- Begin to see your company through the eyes of a buyer.
- Formulate and implement comprehensive sell-side due diligence.

YOUR GOALS AND OBJECTIVES

At the beginning of this section, I posed two questions that the exit plan will address. The first is, "what do you want?" Determining what your goals are as they relate to the sale of your business will help you set a clear course in your exit planning process from day one.

The terms "goals" and "objectives" are tossed around casually in business, but you will benefit from using them with discipline during the exit planning process. So what's the difference?

- A goal is a description of a destination.
- An objective is a measure of the progress that is needed to get to the destination.

Goals are the eventual outcomes you aim to achieve. These goals can be broken into "milestones," or objectives, that are steps along the way. Objectives are often single achievable outcomes. They are concrete in statement and purpose. There is no uncertainty as to whether they have been achieved or not.

By specifying your exact personal goals related to the sale of your company, you are almost certain to identify challenges or obstacles that stand between where you are now and the end state, or goal, toward which you are headed. Knowing this, you then can identify the personal, financial, business, tax, and legal issues you must contend with to complete your journey successfully.

Here are some examples of real business goals from owners we've worked with over the years:

- Retire with X amount in the bank (after tax), which means Y amount paid for my company.
- Receive not less than 85% of the total consideration paid for my company on closing (meaning not more than 15% of the transaction amount being in the form of an earn-out or otherwise).
- Provide my key management team with a bonus of X% of cash received at closing.
- Ensure that my company is placed in the hands of a more capable owner who will realize the company's next growth phase while rewarding my employees with sustainable employment opportunities in a healthy workplace environment.
- Buy my 50-meter yacht and sail around the world.
- Establish a family trust with a minimum of X amount for each of my grandkids.
- Establish a charitable/nonprofit organization to support a cause that my wife and I are passionate about.
- Have enough money to fulfill my life plans but still have X amount left over to pursue a new business venture.
- Preserve the well-being of existing employees, customers, and suppliers.

You can see why exit planning can actually become quite engaging. Once you understand that you are trying to sail around the world or endow a charity, you will be motivated to figure out what you need to do next. This leads you to understanding your objectives—the roadblocks you must overcome to achieve your goals. Typical objectives we've seen include:

- Ensure that financial accounts for last three years are audited by a Big 4 accounting firm.
- Resolve the outstanding lawsuit initiated by a former employee.
- Ensure that a sufficiently qualified, experienced, and capable CEO is ready to assume my position after the transaction.
- Diversify the industry verticals that the business serves.
- Prove the product-market fit of a new product.
- Review and confirm that all proprietary software code is professionally documented.
- Compile as much of the information to be needed in the Due Diligence phase as possible to minimise stress and ensure preparedness.
- Review employment contracts with key staff and, where appropriate, have them enter into new agreements with "stay put" clauses in the event of transfer of ownership.
- Conduct legal analysis to ensure that we own all aspects of our proprietary technology.
- Examine patent protection and, where appropriate, initiate patent applications through an intellectual property law firm.

With your objectives defined, you may find it easier to put all of the other elements involved in the exit planning stage into perspective. Once you have defined the primary objectives and motivating factors behind the sale, it's easier to identify which areas of the business should receive the greatest attention in preparing your business to go to market. Now the path ahead begins to come into focus.

EXAMINING THE OBJECTIVES

There is an array of objectives that almost every business owner must grapple with on their journey to preparing their business for a sale. Here's a quick run-through.

MANAGEMENT SUCCESSION

I know a CEO who prided himself in the fact that he only works two half-days per week, allowing his capable team to fully run the show in his absence and with his complete and utter faith. Consider the buyer's confidence when they ask this CEO the inevitable question: "How reliant is the business on you on a day-to-day basis?"

Remember that throughout the planning and sale process, you must frequently put yourself in the shoes of a buyer. Assess your management team members in the eyes of the investor and if you are not already in the position where you can easily extract yourself from the business on a day-to-day basis, ask yourself who can capably execute your responsibilities in a post-transaction environment. If you're uneasy about their ability, a prospective buyer likely will be, too. Unless you are planning to structure a deal in which you stay on, you're selling the company, not yourself (and even then, you're still selling the company). Potential acquirers must be convinced of a strong supporting management team and will be wary of you leaving the firm if it is overly reliant upon yourself on a daily basis.

It's crucial that you conduct a forthright appraisal to determine if your team possesses (or at the very least, shows potential to possess) the skills to step into your shoes after the sale. If they require further development, you might consider shaping a strategy to help them achieve their potential. This may mean crafting individual plans to help them get there, or even preparing a single individual to assume your role after the sale. If you don't see a strong future for a team member, consider how the potential acquirer will view the situation. You may need to consider replacements if necessary.

The best thing you can do is make yourself redundant long before you commence the process of selling your business. Fail to do this and you risk losing the deal, or at best, receiving a reduced price. You may also face an offer that requires you to remain on for a lengthy period after the transaction, while a replacement is trained in your role.

EMPLOYEE RETENTION

Who are the key employees and how do you expect they will react to a sale? As you must do with the management team, contemplate how you can encourage these people to stay with the company after the transaction. Remember, your buyers will be asking about this. See this from their perspective. How would you want questions about employee retention answered?

Review the employment contracts of key members of your management team. Buyers will certainly inquire about the stability of the management and staff; ensure that your answers instill confidence. You may need to formalize or strengthen key employment agreements. It's worth consulting with a lawyer regarding the inclusion of "stay put" clauses within such agreements, as they help ensure an orderly transition of the business. Nevertheless, the relative value of these agreements depends on the buyer. If you've sold your firm to a buyer who excites your team, they may need little encouragement to remain, as a new owner with a new vision may generate a renewed sense of focus, drive, and enthusiasm for the company's future.

In businesses whose employees are part of a union, it may make sense to renegotiate a new collective bargaining agreement or take other action determined between you and your labor attorney to mitigate the staffing risk that a buyer could face.

THIRD-PARTY RELATIONSHIPS

Ensure that your firm's contracts with third parties, particularly key customers and suppliers, are in place and current. A buyer may ascribe a high value to your customers and/or suppliers. For instance, they may seek to expand their geographical footprint into your region. The demonstrable strength of your customer and supplier relationships will be very important.I always recommend to clients that they consider customer and supplier contract transferability clauses, as this will set the buyer's mind at ease and facilitate a smoother transaction. Clients are sometimes surprised to revisit key contracts with suppliers and customers only to realize that there are onerous change-of-ownership and/or change-of-management clauses. These need to be identified, assessed, and where appropriate, resolved before a sale process commences.

INTELLECTUAL PROPERTY

If your firm has developed intellectual property (IP), then you are aware of the importance of ensuring its protection wherever possible. But have you done so to the best of your ability? Depending on the nature and significance of the IP itself, you may wish to enlist the services of an IP lawyer to ensure that your interests are protected via patents, copyrights, or trademarks. Buyers' confidence quickly erodes when they discover that the IP that they were initially attracted to is insufficiently protected.

In the case of software, for example, you will want to ensure that license contracts do not sacrifice any of the value of your IP, that your code has been stored properly, that you are not leveraging open-source code in a way that lessens your protection, etc.

BUSINESS DOCUMENTATION

All too often, owners neglect general housekeeping tasks such as appropriately organizing key business documents that a new owner would find valuable. The task of ensuring that your company's contracts and records are in order and readily accessible is a relatively quick victory and typically a straightforward exercise in good administration. More involved—and likely requiring the attention of your senior team—is documenting key processes, procedures, and methodologies. Remember—if you bought this business, what would you want to know? Think HR manuals, maintenance routines, insurance renewals, health and safety policies, and new employee intake processes. Approach this with the objective of creating confidence in the buyer during the due diligence process.

SKELETONS IN THE CLOSET

What surprises lie in wait? Is there a disgruntled employee who may sue? A pending regulatory change that you may need to adjust to? A lien on your building? Don't surprise your potential buyer. Find these problems and address them as effectively as you can. If you can't fix them, be sure you disclose them early on in the process. Trust is an important component in the process of closing a sale. Surprises, especially unpleasant ones revealed late in the process, only erode that trust.

BUSINESS VALUATION

As I described in Chapter 2, valuation is both a science and an art, with an element of subjectivity added in. If you skipped over that chapter, flip back for a discussion of the factors that go into valuation.

VALUE DRIVER ANALYSIS

What makes your company desirable for a potential buyer? Understanding the qualities that make it unique and appealing helps you see your firm from a buyer's point of view. Again, refer to Chapter 2 for a more detailed discussion.

VALUE ENHANCEMENT OPPORTUNITIES

What can—and what should—you do to maximize your company's value? This sort of work doesn't happen overnight, and may take months to complete. Opportunities are either strategic or tactical.

STRATEGIC

The right customers can be a vital component in determining your company's value. Many buyers purchase firms in order to gain access to the seller's customers. Look at your customer mix. What is the ideal mix to make the business attractive? Revenue concentration detracts from value—what if you lose a major customer (or supplier)? How resilient will the firm be in such an event? Build a customer mix that defends the firm against uncontrolled outside events, such as the bankruptcy or acquisition of a customer or supplier.

What's your business model? Do you get your revenue from one-off transactions, or is it recurring revenue? The latter adds more value, so if that's part of your revenue mix, focus on it.

Are you planning to roll out new products or services? Most buyers won't ascribe value to pipeline products, so go ahead and get them out in the marketplace. Prove their value. The exceptions are in areas such as complex tech and pharma, wherein buyers will look at what's in the pipeline more closely.

TACTICAL

Address any potential due diligence items that could reduce valuation or even kill the deal. Many private companies engage in activity that is reasonable for a closely held company, but could be a problem for a publicly traded buyer or one with a dispersed shareholder base. Examples include related-party transactions or running personal or family expenses or assets through the company.

Clean up your books and balance sheets. Get a third-party review, and consider whether an audit makes sense and what you need to do to bring the books into alignment with Generally Accepted Accounting Principles (GAAP).

EXIT OPTIONS ANALYSIS

Who should buy your business? You can't effectively answer that question until you have a clear vision of what you want—of what's right for you and your co-shareholders. Here are the common options most sellers consider:

- Outright or partial sale to a third party, with or without a competitive bidding process
- Corporate partnerships or joint ventures
- Selling the company to employees—employee stock ownership plan (ESOP)
- An initial public offering (IPO)
- Selling/transferring ownership to family members

If you're not planning to keep your company in your family, then it's most likely you're interested in selling to a third party. This book focuses primarily on that option—selling to a strategic or financial buyer—but I'll briefly touch on the other options here.

SALE OR TRANSFER TO FAMILY MEMBERS

A sale or transfer of your business to the next generation is frequently an issue of estate planning rather than structuring a transaction. How and when you will hand over management control to the next generation is also a primary concern with this exit option.

ADVANTAGES
- Attractive tax advantages may be realized with proper planning
- Permits your family members to enjoy the fruits of your labor
- Nominal cultural disruption (usually)
- As the founder and/or owner, your legacy lives on
- May provide opportunity for involvement of other key managers

DISADVANTAGES
- Depending on your tax jurisdiction, the tax authorities may scrutinize family transfers of ownership
- Tax authorities may demand evidence that the transaction price was realistic
- The price paid by a family member is almost certainly lower than the "best owner" described previously
- Estate transfer may require significant funding for estate tax

INITIAL PUBLIC OFFERING

An Initial Public Offering (IPO) is a high-profile, even sexy way to sell your business. It is not, however, a full exit for most founders. And it is not a practical route for most family and privately owned companies. An IPO is better described as a capital-raising event than an optimal-liquidity event. Taking a company public typically enables an owner to free up only a share of his/her personal wealth in the short to medium term. A full exit by way of an IPO may require many years or may fail ever to be fully achieved. Given the complexities of today's financial markets and heavy costs of exchange-listed status, an owner should carefully consider whether the public market option is the most logical in light of other alternatives.

ADVANTAGES

- Provides access to long-term capital
- Improves financial position
- Provides some liquidity for shareholders
- Prestige and public awareness
- Increases ability to attract and retain key personnel via stock options

DISADVANTAGES

- IPOs are nearly always underpriced, often to the tune of 20%+ (the most pertinent reason is that the bankers and PR agents want the offering to be "over-subscribed," meaning that there are more investors wanting to buy stock than shares available)
- Lack of operating confidentiality
- Strict compliance requirements and high compliance costs (such as Sarbanes-Oxley in the United States)
- Pressure for short-term performance
- Reduced business flexibility
- Executive compensation scrutiny
- Potential liability to public shareholders

CORPORATE PARTNERSHIPS OR JOINT VENTURES

An otherwise appropriate buyer may not be interested in buying because your business is not in a high-growth phase, yet you have an established position in a certain market that is attractive. Alternatively, a potential partner may be a foreign company that is seeking a presence in your jurisdiction, but does not want an ownership stake, or is not yet ready to fully commit to entering a new geographical market and wants to test the waters first.

A partnership or joint venture can be a valid growth strategy to consider if you and another business identify mutual synergies but also find reasons not to consummate a complete purchase at the moment, if ever.

ADVANTAGES
- Can offer access to new markets
- Sharing of technology, people, material supply, and capacity
- Opportunity for deeper relationships with customers
- Opportunity for expanded product offerings
- Opportunity to acquire partners or to be acquired in a two-step process

DISADVANTAGES
- Complicated to set up, particularly when considering all potential scenarios that may unfold in the future between the parties
- Can prove difficult to sustain long term
- Partners may not be contributing equally or may have inequality in economic leverage and strength
- The needs and interests of the parties can change at any time

STRATEGIC TIMING

Once your business is ready to go to market, decide whether now is the time. Micro and macro business cycles can significantly affect valuation. A good example is steel. When the industry is hot and supplies of steel are low, investors will be looking to buy steel companies. When the market takes a downturn—and steel can be very cyclical—interest among investors drops substantially.

TAX AND NET PROCEEDS CALCULATION

Consult with your accountant to ensure a tax-efficient strategy is developed and implemented. You'll want to be sure that you are set up flexibly, able to accept a range of deal types without causing your financial stress or requiring your team to be excessively creative to avoid an unnecessary tax burden.

CHAPTER 4

CHOOSING THE RIGHT
M&A ADVISOR

"A fool despises good counsel, but a wise man takes it to heart."

—Confucius

Just as every team needs a coach (that's you), every team also needs a captain who will lead the team in executing the coach's strategy. He or she will handle much of the day-to-day work on your behalf—after all, you still have a business to run. In most cases, the captain of the team is your M&A advisor. They will execute the overwhelming majority of the responsibilities associated with selling the business. Choosing the right advisor for you and your business is consequently one of the most vital tasks you face.

Your advisor's key role is to package and market your business for sale, and see that sale through to the best global investor, based on your goals and exit planning. A good M&A advisor brings with him the experience of completing many deals. He can assume an overarching view on the end-to-end process that other professionals in transactions cannot. When the deal falls apart (and they usually do at some point), a qualified and experienced M&A advisor is the one who can take a wider view, working with the seller's and buyer's teams to rediscover common ground and ensure the deal is put back on track—and that it stays on track until a successful conclusion.

You must be confident that your advisor will provide professional guidance on how to effectively market and position your company to a targeted group of international investors; how to position the synergistic value drivers with investors; to whom and how aggressively to market it; how they will keep you well informed throughout; how to develop meaningful dialogues with each investor party; who their team will be and who will be your main point of contact; how they will proceed with negotiations; how they will manage expressions of interest received, and so on.

In **The Exit Academy**, my 11½ hour on-demand online video training course that I've created as a continuation of this book, I speak in great detail about the importance of these factors. And I do that for one simple reason: it's extremely important that business owners know how business transactions are most effectively marketed, positioned, negotiated and closed in today's world. It really is that *critical for you*, the business owner, to understand this *before* you embark upon your exit journey so that you can be sure to choose the advisor that's right for you (you can learn more about The Exit Academy at *www.markcarmichael.com*).

M&A ADVISORS VS. INVESTMENT BANKERS VS. BUSINESS BROKERS

The major determinant in whether you will work with a business broker, an M&A advisor, or an investment banker is deal size.

- Business brokers: Typical transaction size is less than $2-$5 million.

- Investment banker: Typical transaction size is greater than $250 million (although deal sizes can be lower, provided their minimum success fee threshold is met).

- M&A advisor: Typical transaction size is between $5+ million and $250+ million (though advisor deal sizes can be much larger than $250 million).

BUSINESS BROKERS

Brokers usually work with smaller companies that are purchased by an individual, rather than a corporate or institutional buyer. Their process is similar to selling a home, and many business brokers are often real estate agents as well. Typically, business brokers sell companies that are income replacement for the owner-operator. Valuation is based on a multiple of the "seller's discretionary earnings"—that is, the cash flows generated by the business to the owner-operator. The broker assembles information regarding the business and advertises the company on business-for-sale websites with an asking price. The typical transaction structure is an asset sale (the sale of the company's assets) using a template or standard forms.

INVESTMENT BANKERS

Insofar as mergers and acquisitions are concerned, M&A advisors and investment bankers are somewhat interchangeable, with a few key differences. Investment bankers characteristically work with larger corporate clients and offer a wider range of services than M&A advisors. These can include initial public offerings (IPOs), fairness opinions, raising capital for clients through securities operations in the equity and debt markets, and structuring complex and sophisticated financial products. Investment bankers typically charge fees considerably higher than M&A advisors. It is not atypical for an investment bank to have minimum success fees of $3 million or more, which dictates the minimum size client they can serve.

M&A ADVISORS

M&A advisors bridge the market gap between transactions that are clearly led by investment bankers and those managed by business brokers. M&A advisors are typically more consultative and often work with clients in the strategy and planning phases as they consider their options regarding an exit. Both M&A advisors and investment bankers run a sophisticated process to sell a company that is proactive and usually focused on creating a competitive bidding situation among interested acquirers. This contrasts with the passive, more simplistic process implemented by business brokers. The actively managed process of M&A advisors and investment bankers tends to add considerable value, equating to a higher price achieved for the seller's business. A business owner should expect the work of a good M&A advisor to pay for itself.

THINK MARKETING

All qualified advisors are proficient with numbers—that's a minimum requirement to be in the business, not a reason to select someone. When it comes to choosing an advisor, think "marketing." An advisor has to do many things, but the most important is to create a situation in which multiple qualified bidders vie for your company. This competitive bidding environment is going to happen only if the advisor markets your company effectively. Far too many advisors of all stripes are astonishingly unaware of the importance of conducting a thorough marketing and outreach process, or incapable of doing so. For large companies with a limited number of possible buyers, a wide-reaching marketing program isn't needed. Smaller- to mid-sized companies, let's call them firms with valuations in the $10 million to $250 million range, however, directly benefit from marketing because statistics show that in about 75% of middle-market deals, the seller didn't know the buyer prior to the deal. In the middle market, using the Internet and making a dozen phone calls isn't enough.

Here are the characteristics that a potential advisor should be able to communicate to you:

- Unflagging energy and enthusiasm for selling your company

- Accomplished and sophisticated international marketing and selling capabilities
- A record of accomplishments
- Intelligent research and persistent investor engagement
- Keen negotiators
- Legal acumen
- International outreach
- Likeable and responsible
- Can identify and position strategic synergies with investors

Focus on identifying those attributes. Recognize that the first questions that come to mind likely will be the wrong questions. For example, we have been asked, "Have you sold a gold mine before?" "What transactions have you done for solar panel manufacturers?" "How many casinos have you sold?"

Contrary to what many advisors would have you think, having sold a company in a related field is seldom a justifiable reason for choosing that advisor.

You may own a particularly specialized business. Selling it may require specific expertise. The question to ask a potential advisor in this case is not "have you ever sold a business such as mine?" Rather, ask how they will acquire the expertise needed to sell your firm effectively. We were once engaged to sell a pharmaceutical company that had produced two highly sophisticated drugs that were in trial phases (i.e., no sales). The client wanted us to have a drug expert on the team. Not surprisingly, we didn't have one in house. Instead, we retained the services of one of the United States' great drug developers, along with a former director of the Food & Drug Administration, to fill the gap.

Advisors don't need to be experts in every industry sector. They need to know how to sell your business. The best M&A advisors invest heavily in the process of marketing: exhaustively researching potential buyers, building an investment thesis as to why your firm would be a suitable acquisition target for them, identifying the appropriate individuals within each target company, and so forth. Their objective is to identify and effectively contact (not so easy—more on this below) "best owner" candidates who can realize maximum value from your firm, and thus will bring the most to the table.

Given that the quality of the investor list largely determines the overall success of the process (think quality in, quality out—or conversely, garbage in, garbage out), you owe it to yourself and shareholders to ensure that your advisor has an implicit knowledge of how to market and sell your company. That starts with, among other things, the quality of the investor universe the advisor has identified and selected to become part of the outreach to find the right buyer. If an advisor says, "we know all the right buyers for your business," start looking for the door. No advisor knows that until he or she has done the work of casting a wide net. Your advisor should do this using proprietary databases (usually built over a number of years) and similar M&A research tools that are often quite expensive, but are essential to developing a robust, global universe of qualified investors.

Perhaps you want to run a highly selective outreach campaign, preferring to minimize the potential for the market (your customers, suppliers, and competitors) to know that you're considering selling. In such a case, a limited outreach may be the best option, but it still must start with identifying the global pool of investors, assessing each, and arriving at the short list of those parties you and your advisor believe have the ability to transact. It's a labor-intensive process, but necessary to ensure the highest probability of success. At my firm, we typically plan to spend more than 100 man-hours conducting research before arriving at this short list.

Whether your strategy is the short-list approach or a more expansive approach (I highly recommend the expansive approach wherever possible, as you're likely to have more bidders taking a seat at the negotiation table), the same effort is required. We devote the long man-hours to ensure that we've identified the global pool of investors who would likely have an interest in our client's business.

Unfortunately, many advisors cut corners here, skimping on time, money, or energy. They may rely instead on business-for-sale websites, member-driven M&A associations (wherein they can promote the sale of your business to hundreds of other M&A firms in the hope that one or more will have an interested buyer), or they carry out an investor outreach program based on a rented database or similarly unsophisticated approach.

EFFECTIVE MARKETING

Once an advisor has identified the best targets, they must possess the ability and experience to convincingly present and promote your company. A fundamental component of this process is the investor marketing materials that have been prepared by your advisor. The point of the marketing materials should not be to sell your company—but unfortunately, not every advisor realizes this. We've seen 100-plus page documents that have been sent as part of a cold call e-mail (in case you're wondering who reads such documents, the answer is: no one) that give away far too much information—just the sort of content your competitors would love to get their hands on.

Don't randomly give away proprietary information on your company. We've seen documents that were effectively the seller's "playbook," containing overly detailed and sensitive information related to customers, margins, lawsuits, current strategy, etc. Consider carefully the content of the marketing materials and always remember that the more in-depth/sensitive information can be distributed as discussions with an investor as they progress into the more advanced stages.

The purpose of the Information Memorandum (the key document in your outreach, also referred to as "IM") is to pique the target's interest and motivate them to pick up the phone. The most effective IMs are reasonably brief (not more than 25 pages or so), and are professionally written and designed. Where appropriate, the content within is customized to each recipient, highlighting the relevant synergies or other compelling points of your business that would be of interest to the reader (this is where the research on each target comes into play).

A good way to determine if your potential advisor cuts corners is to look at past marketing materials, such as their outreach communications. Do they seem generic or unprofessionally written? If so, that's usually a bad sign.

Here's an example of what I mean about an ineffective communication; in this case, it's an e-mail introduction:

> *Dear Sir, our client, a pharmaceutical distribution company with revenues of $60m and offices in the United States and Germany, is seeking an investor to acquire 100% of the shares in its business…and we thought you might be interested…."*

If the M&A advisor has built a well-researched investor target list, developed an investment thesis for each target, and identified the correct individual to contact, the e-mail should look more like this:

> *George,*
>
> *Our client is an international pharmaceutical distribution company with offices in the United States and Germany and revenues of $60m USD. We are contacting you for the following reasons:*
>
> *1. We believe that ABC may be an ideal acquirer of our client's business due to your firm's strategic initiative to enter the German market. Our client has a long-standing presence in Germany, inclusive of*

established distribution, numerous blue-chip clients, and a solid client list, including several of Germany's leading hospitals and health care centers. This acquisition may prove a highly effective entry for ABC into the German market.

2. Our client has the exclusive distribution rights to XYZ product in Germany. Given that your firm also has the exclusive rights for this product to North America, and given XYZ's consistent global sales growth, we felt that as Head of M&A for ABC you would find this an attractive opportunity..."

Can you see the enhanced impact that the latter e-mail would have on George, as compared to the former? Yet the standard industry outreach looks more like the first e-mail: generic statements that apply no knowledge about the potential investor they are contacting or why the offer would be of interest to them, and make absolutely no attempt to connect on a personal level with the recipient.

"WHAT'S YOUR PROCESS?"

Confirm the advisor's process to better understand how disciplined they are in each step and further, how disciplined they are at talking you through each step.

Many cut corners in the process, which has the inevitable result of poor outcomes. If they don't have depth in their internal team, the danger of cutting corners is particularly concerning, as they simply do not have the resource to address all the areas appropriately in selling your firm. Areas of deficiency often include:

- Not devoting the time and energy to identify, research, understand, and secure the appropriate contact details of each potential buyer in the universe of potential investors;

- Failing to develop professional marketing materials that will make the right first impression and compel the reader to want to learn more;

- Failing to market and sell your firm with the passion, resource commitment, and experience required;

- Inexperienced negotiators acting on your behalf in discussions with buyers; and

- Failure to lead to successful conclusion from initial expression of interest through the due diligence and drafting of transaction documents stages.

We have seen these all happen—countless times—with other advisors.

To avoid these outcomes, query a potential advisor on the depth of their process:

- *Can they show you a documented process?* If they can't do this to your satisfaction, head for the door.

- *When they talk you through each step of the process, how do you feel?* Does their explanation make you feel comfortable and informed? If not, pay attention to that feeling. Similarly, do you actually like them? If they come across as arrogant or condescending, that same feeling will almost certainly be conveyed to investors when they are speaking or meeting with them.

- *Do they keep detailed notes during the marketing phase?* You will want to be able to confirm how many times they've reached out to buyers (and how—by phone, e-mail, in person) and the feedback they've received.

- *How do they summarize this information for you and how often?*

At the end of the day, this is your business that you're selling. Suffice it to say that you have the right to ask every question you see fit to ask to develop a comprehensive understanding of how the advisor is going to act on your behalf. If they are passionate, detailed, and convincing in talking you through each step of the process, are ensuring that they are answering your questions to your satisfaction and are intelligent, capable and likeable people, then you are on the right track.

You can email me at *ExitSupport@markcarmichael.com* to request a list of questions to use when qualifying advisors.

ONE IS NOT ENOUGH

Skillful outreach requires experience, the investment of time and energy, good process, dedication, deal-making ability, and thick skin, if it is to be done right. And this is an area that you want done right. Period.

Multiple contacts within each target company are particularly important. You want to ensure that the right person(s) within each firm is aware of the opportunity to acquire your company. We know through experience that pitching two to three specific individuals within a firm increases the probability of a successful discussion with the firm in question by 39%.

In 2013, we conducted an exercise throughout the year that we named "Champion/Challenger." The Champion was our control strategy, the approach we had most often implemented in outreach, which was to identify the person who we determined was the most appropriate individual to approach regarding an acquisition opportunity for their firm. The Challenger was the test strategy in which we identified, on average, two and a half contacts per company. This was the only difference between the Champion and the Challenger.

After identifying the target companies to be approached, we then split them on an A/B basis, meaning that the first contact was a Champion, while the second was a Challenger, and so on down the list of target companies.

In order to ensure statistical significance, we ran this test across a multitude of outreach campaigns across the year, totaling 2,148 contacts in all for the test. In the end, the Challenger proved 39% more successful in establishing a meaningful dialogue with target companies (we identified "meaningful" as establishing a direct dialogue with at least one individual within that firm, even if the outcome of that dialogue was negative—i.e., "we're not interested"). Simply put, by increasing the number of suitable targets within each company from one to two and a half, the rate of successful engagement increased by 39%.

Ensure that your advisor has a specific view on outreach that will generate the highest probability of success. Too often, advisors send a pitch to a single person in a firm. Worse yet, many will simply send to "info@.....com" with the subject heading of "Please forward on to your Business Development Director." Ask to see some of your potential advisor's pitch e-mails, and pay attention to whom they were addressed.

Finally, don't ever let an advisor commence investor out-reach until you have given written approval on the list of targets. There may be unfriendly competitors, valuable cus-tomers, or others on their list that you don't want to know about your plans. Even worse, you don't want to give com-petitors the opportunity to gain valuable insight into your company by posing as a potentially interested acquirer.

KNOW THE TEAM

The M&A advisor is a key member of your deal team, but of course an advisor is a company made up of individuals. You want to be assured that your deal is getting the attention, energy, and focus it requires. Develop an understanding of the depth of the team you're engaging: their educa-tion, age, backgrounds, and experience. Determine who will be working on your deal and how the team dedicated to you will divide those roles and responsibilities.

Behind the scenes of a sell-side engagement, there is a flurry of ongoing activity. Each advisor will have varying approaches, so I've summarized how we address and assign the responsibilities of a sell-side mandate with in my firm, STS Capital Partners, , as this provides a thorough understand-ing for you to use in your discussions with your prospective advisor.

Deal Leadership
- This is the individual who assumes ultimate ownership from beginning to end of executing the full strategy, leading to a successful closing. This individual is your main point of con-tact throughout the process and is often the leader of advanced negotiations with investors as well as the key dealmaker. In deals that me and my team lead, the Deal Leader is always myself.

Research

- Conduct international analysis to identify potential strategic and financial buyers.
- Build an investment thesis for each potential buyer, positioning the seller's company most effectively with each target.
- Carry out industry research on the sector in which the client operates, identifying recent trends and political, environmental, societal and technology changes within the sector that may influence the marketing strategy.

Database Management

- Enter all qualified prospective investors and all contact details into the database.
- Provide daily updates on discussions with prospective investors, noting comments/feedback/objections, setting alarms for follow-up calls/meetings, etc.

Financial Analysis

- Develop a detailed financial understanding of the seller's business.
- Develop financial models to be used in Confidential Information Memorandum.
- Calculate and negotiate working capital requirements.
- Develop responses to any investor-based financial analysis used in determining value of business.

Investor Communications

- First-Tier Communications = Outreach Team
  - Initiate contact with investor, gauge initial level of interest, negotiate and enter into confidentiality agreement, send Information Memorandum, follow up to gauge interest and escalate to second-tier communications.

- Second-Tier Communications = Deal Lead Team
  - Commence deeper discussions about seller's business, assess mutual fit, determine qualifications of the potential investor, build rapport, advance conversations, distribute supplemental marketing documents to enrich discussions, initiate talks around valuation, position client's business valuation parameters (speak from position of factual evidence to support valuation parameters), determine synergies between client business and investor business, elicit written expressions of interest from investor.

- Advanced-Tier Communications = Deal Lead Team
  - Negotiate formal Letters of Intent (LOIs)

  - Support exclusivity/data room phase info requests and questions from buyer(s)

  - Ensure continued progress in all facets

  - Play key role in drafting of definitive agreements by inserting themselves into lawyer discussions to ensure continued progress

Marketing Materials Production
- Work with research and analysis team to prepare Confidential Information Memorandum, teaser, and all supplemental presentation documents.
- Ensure compelling storyline throughout all marketing documents.
- Oversee graphic design and layout of marketing materials.

Contracts Management
- Review/negotiate and execute non-disclosure agreement changes proposed by potential investors.

- Provide internal review on Letters of Interest, all aspects of definitive purchase agreements.
- Assist team on all aspects of definitive purchase agreements.

Administration

- Fulfill general administrative requirements, billings, banking issues, etc.

Who, specifically, will be doing what? All too often, a senior member of the advisory firm pitches you for your business, gains your trust and confidence, and signs the dotted line with you. Then you discover that he or she has little to do with the actual work. You want to be assured—in writing, if that makes you sleep easier—of whom your key team members will be throughout. You will be spending a lot of time with them; the last thing you want is to discover that key aspects of the process have been handed to someone you don't particularly care for, or worse, a junior with little experience. Make sure you know who your team is going to be.

That said, it is not unreasonable for junior members to form part of the team. They can add significant value in assisting with research, data-basing investor call notes, doing basic follow up, and so on. Don't be surprised if a few associates are part of your team. The main point is that those doing the heavy lifting of researching, contacting, and negotiating with potential buyers are the right individuals.

SELECTING YOUR ADVISOR

You hire an M&A advisor to create incremental value via a process, so make sure they have an established track record of doing so. Selling your business can be a long, demanding process, with challenges and conflicts to work through. The best way to gain insight here is to understand their deal experience, and their track record for achieving successful results for companies like yours.

Here are some specific questions to ask.

What is their deal experience? Develop an understanding of what types of deals they've done recently, where, in what industries and in what price range. Where were the clients based? The buyers? Have them provide an overview or case study of a few recent transactions. They may not be able to disclose the name or transaction details of the client due to confidentiality agreements, but they should be able to walk you through a comprehensive summary of the process.

Inquire about their current, recent, and upcoming engagements. This will give you insight into whether they truly operate on an international basis, the types of clients they are working with, and the size of companies they represent. You may want to think twice if their average deal size is one-tenth the size of your anticipated transaction value. We've come across our fair share of business brokers who present themselves as M&A advisors in an effort to attract larger clients. Also, the number of clients that a certain M&A team will take on at one time gives insight into how much time they will spend on your project. If the advisor has only a modest sized team and has 10 sell-side clients at a time, it's highly likely that they perform a more cursory sale process.

A lot of sellers—and advisors alike—look for completed transactions in the industry of the seller's business. As I mentioned previously, while I understand that impulse, I believe it is, in most cases, misdirected. Sellers who pursue this line of questioning tend to assume that if an advisor has completed deals in their sector, that advisor will have meaningful industry contacts and deeper insight into who is actively making acquisitions. This thinking is flawed for three reasons. First, unless the deal was completed very recently—within the last few months—the relationships they have built are likely to have eroded, people have changed jobs, the firms they know have changed their growth strategy, and so on. Second, the way to find out who is actively making acquisitions is by executing a comprehensive global outreach campaign. Not by relying on who's in your address book. Finally, if the advisor does multiple deals per year with the same limited group of buyers, where do you think their loyalty will be? In other words, when discussions progress to advanced negotiations, will they be prepared to take a more aggressive position in negotiating the best deal on your behalf—potentially putting their long-established relationships with such buyers in jeopardy?

What is their marketing process? Ask each candidate about the details of their buyer research and buyer outreach process. They should not hesitate in providing you with a robust answer. If they do, or if they appear uncertain how to answer the question, that's a red flag. In the M&A world, there are many—and I mean *many*—who would have you believe that they possess the skills to deliver the result you require. All too often, their approach is little more than what a real estate agent would employ in selling your house.

Can they negotiate well? This is not a hard-and-fast assessment. Ask the advisor some straightforward questions: How do you negotiate? What is your strategy? Who oversees negotiations? What experience do you have negotiating?

More generally, look for characteristics that indicate a potentially good negotiator. These include:

- Likability/ability to generate rapport;
- Logical way of thinking and approaching an issue;
- Professional, conscientious, and detail-oriented when appropriate;
- Ability to deal with conflict without emotion; and

- Comfortable with any grey areas and ability to understand both sides of an issue.

Along the same lines, the Massachusetts Institute of Technology (MIT) identified these characteristics of a good negotiator, some of which you can assess in conversation:

- Preparation and planning skill
- Knowledge of the subject matter being negotiated
- Ability to think clearly and rapidly under pressure and uncertainty
- Ability to express thoughts verbally
- Listening skill
- Judgment and general intelligence
- Integrity
- Ability to persuade others
- Patience
- Decisiveness
- Considers lots of options
- Is aware of the process and style of the other person
- Flexibility
- Thinks and talks about possible areas of agreement

What resources do they have available? Many business owners hire an advisor without knowing much about them, only to later discover that the firm is a one- or two-man firm. Now that you're developing a sense of the enormous resource commitment required to develop, implement, and execute a comprehensive international sell-side process, it's easy to see that to do it effectively you need a well-resourced team.

Professional advisory firms will have a team comprised of directors, researchers, investor outreach, database management, legal/contracts, financial analysts, and financial model experts and more. Have them include a breakdown of the specific resources they employ and ask whether these are full-time employees or third parties contracted on an as-needed basis. In the end, you want to develop a sense of the firm and their ability to get the job done; an understanding of who they are and what commitment they have to delivering the successful result for you.

Does your advisor have a potential conflict of interest? Owners of mid-market to larger firms may be approached by investment banks. This sort of attention may be flattering, particularly if the bank is bringing a lot of expertise and resources to the table. However, be wary. Investment banks may create fee structures that misalign the incentives between the client and the advisor. Potentially more problematic is that in some cases the bank may have an existing relationship with a potential buyer. They could end up being paid on both sides of the deal—and the seller never thinks to ask.

Check references from recent transactions. Contact a couple of the firm's clients and discuss these areas with them:

- Integrity—Did the firm act with professional integrity and give honest, objective advice? Were they willing to deliver bad news as well as good?
- Knowledge—Did the firm have a good understanding of accounting and financial principals throughout the transaction? Did they take the time to learn about your business?
- Experience—Did they bring experience to bear on the process? Who were the main points of contact throughout—junior associates, or principals?
- Communication—Did the firm's employees communicate well orally and in writing? Did they keep the client informed throughout the process?
- Negotiation—Did they display negotiation skills to structure the best deal for the seller?

- Marketing—Did they perform a thorough global search? Were their marketing materials effective? Did they develop an investment thesis for each target?

- Persistence—Not all deals proceed smoothly, so it can take persistence to get a deal done.

Don't act too hastily. Take time to get to know and get comfortable with the firm. A reputable advisor who is genuinely interested in selling your company will invest significantly in the initial discussions. They should show that they genuinely want to understand your objectives and goals, and to develop an in-depth understanding of your company and the sector in which you operate. If they're not asking you insightful questions throughout, consider this an indication of either lack of interest or lack of sophistication. In either case, this is likely not the right advisor for you.

If you're not yet sure about whether to sell your business, be honest. Tell the advisor that you're considering a sale but are not yet convinced that it's the right thing to do, so you're seeking advice. Any respectable advisor will be happy to engage with you on this basis. Finally, no credible advisor should ask you to pay for advice or anything else until you have a clear commitment to selling your business.

TERMS OF ENGAGEMENT

The engagement letter entered into between your company and your advisor is vital. Properly structured, it aligns your and your advisor's interests so that the advisor is properly incentivized to close a deal for you at the highest price and on the best deal terms. Below are several of the most decisive points to cover in your agreement. Your deal lawyer (see the next chapter) can assist you in ensuring all the necessary points are covered in your letter of engagement with your advisor.

EXCLUSIVITY

Most reputable M&A advisors will require exclusivity, for mutually beneficial reasons. An advisor is going to invest a substantial amount of time, money, effort, opportunity cost and analysis into preparing your company for sale and leading your exit process. This means several months of full-time work. A credible advisor isn't going to take such a project on, nor make the necessary investment, without a reasonable expectation of a payout at the end.

There's a reason you as a business owner should want exclusivity, too. If you have more than one advisor working to sell your business you can end up in an uncomfortable and potentially costly situation. Consider the following scenario of two non-exclusive advisors, Bob and John:

- Bob is negotiating with two investors on your behalf.
- John is negotiating with three investors on your behalf.
- Bob tells his investors, "If your offer is $40 million, you will be in the lead and likely to secure the deal."
- However, Bob is unaware that John has positioned the opportunity with his investors at $45 million.
- Thus, the investor working with Bob submits an offer for $40 million, only to later learn that another advisor, John, has brought in a Letter of Intent pegging the price at $45 million.
- Bob winds up embarrassed and looking unprofessional. His investor is feeling misled and irate at wasting time and money for the $40 million bid.

- The bottom line for you? Bob's investor is feeling burned and not likely to view you, or your company, in a good light. If the $45 million deal doesn't go through (quite common), you'll wish you had that unhappy investor as a backup.

  Furthermore, two advisors may engage the same investor. Who gets the success fee? I have seen this play out a few times over the years and in both cases, both advisors made the argument to the seller that they would expect their success fee should that investor conclude a transaction.

Quality advisors take each mandate very seriously. If an agreement is not exclusive, or if it can be cancelled at any time without consideration, an advisor will not be incentivized to invest appropriately in the project.

FEE STRUCTURE

Fees are an obvious and important factor to consider when choosing your M&A advisor and often misunderstood. Because there are significant differences in the fees advisory firms charge, many sellers largely base their selection criteria on the disparity. However, as with everything in life, you generally get what you pay for. You may strike a deal that minimizes your fees, but also shortchanges you on the level of sophistication employed and limited scope of services and effort you receive. A higher fee is entirely justified if you end up with a more successful outcome. Regardless of what you pay, what matters is ensuring the fee structure keeps your advisor properly incentivized to work in your best interest.

The fee structure is very important to both you and your advisor, as it determines how your advisor will be compensated, and thus their incentives. Advisors characteristically divide their fees into two parts:

1. An Engagement/Work/Retainer Fee;
2. A Success Fee.

THE RETAINER

The retainer (also referred to as an Engagement Fee, Work Fee or Retainer Fee) is often a point of some discussion. It can be set up as a fixed fee payable at the beginning of the engagement; a fee structure payable as certain milestones are achieved; or a flat monthly fee. In my experience, the most common is a monthly fee as it is easier for the seller to budget for.

Have a conversation with your advisor about what, precisely, the retainer covers. Some advisors will pad the retainer not only to cover their costs, but also to ensure that a profit is realized, even if they are unsuccessful in selling your business. The best firms, in my opinion, seek only to cover a portion of their costs directly associated with carrying out the work being done on your behalf. The principle at work here is to give both sides a real incentive to close the deal. If the deal doesn't close, the advisor loses real money. As a result, you and the advisor are both investing in the process and thus, both aligned to conclude a successful deal.

We adopted this approach a number of years back. We calculate the estimated costs to be incurred during the period of our mandate with a client, then propose to the client that these monthly costs be split on a 50/50 basis. This distributes the financial commitment evenly across my firm and the client. The client can see that we are clearly investing real money into the sale process and that if we do not drive a deal across the line, we have incurred a considerable loss, both monetarily and in terms of opportunity cost. We are aligned.

Equally, when the owner agrees to pay a retainer, he is signaling that he's serious about selling his business and is willing to invest in the process.

There are numerous resources you can source online regarding what an appropriate retainer fee should be. Much of the information as it relates to what is an appropriate retainer fee, success fee and/or the terms one should expect to be included in an engagement agreement between seller and advisor may at first appear contradicting. The reason for that is most commonly due to the fact that each sell-side mandate is unique in nature and requires an advisor to understand and assess the variables to be addressed in each of the phases of an exit process that lead to a successful closing.

Factors to be considered by an M&A advisor when assessing a new potential sell-side client include:

- Transaction size;
- Deal complexity;
- Readiness of the seller for an exit; is his/her business prepared for an exit;
- Legal implications;
- Recent financial performance of the business;
- Overall macro-economic factors that may positively/negatively impact the sale process;
- Geographical/Jurisdictional/Geopolitical factors;
- Alignment (or lack thereof) amongst shareholders as to the willingness to sell;
- Shareholder disagreements regarding valuation expectations;
- Timing expectations;
- Marketability/overall attractiveness of the business being sold;

Factoring in the above provides the advisor with a reasonable estimate as to the resources they will need to commit and the resulting estimated internal costs incurred. From there, they can make an informed estimate to include in their proposal to you. In a recent survey conducted by Firmex in 2021, 47% of those surveyed reported charging monthly retainers of between $5,000-$15,000 per month; 17% charge more than $15,000 per month; 26% charged less than $5,000 per month.

THE SUCCESS FEE

The success fee typically is expressed as a percentage of the overall transaction value and is paid to the advisor at closing. Whenever I speak at entrepreneur or CEO events, questions related to success fees always arise—and with valid reason, as there are rumors and misperceptions regarding high fees, uncertainty as to the advisor's role, whether they need an advisor or not, and so on. The result is that the business owner often underestimates or doesn't understand the value a qualified advisor can bring to a transaction. The concern regarding fees versus the value delivered by the advisor are often at the top of the list of concerns.

A qualified advisor is hired to add incremental value to the process, to maximize the probability of a successful transaction and further, to ensure that the absolute best deal is secured on your behalf. The success fee is their incentive to work very long hours, often seven days a week, to deliver the goal of selling your business.

Success fees come in many different forms and structures can vary considerably from one advisor to the next and from one sell-side mandate to the next, including:

- Fixed percentage of the overall transaction value: Advisor and client agree to a fixed percentage paid to advisor at closing of the overall transaction value; as value increases, so too does the associated success fee amount. This clause creates a compelling motivation for the advisor to ensure not simply that the deal closes, but that the highest valuation is realized, often exceeding the seller's original pricing expectations;

- Scaled percentage structure: Scaled success fee percentages are used in 40-50% of sell-side mandates and are based on a determined transaction value (or enterprise value) and coinciding success fee percentage for a transaction completed at this valuation. If the realised transaction value exceeds the set valuation, an increase in the success fee is paid to the advisor by the seller. In such circumstances, the incentive is for the M&A advisor to exceed the seller's expectations, earning successively higher fees. For example, the seller and M&A advisor may agree to a 5% fee for a transaction up to X valuation, with the next 10 million earning a success fee of 8%, the following 10 million earning 10%, etc.

- Lehman formula: Developed in the early 1970s, it became an accepted formula through the 1990s, as it was a 5-4-3-2-1 tiered structure, meaning:
  - 5% of the first $1 million
  - 4% of the second $1 million
  - 3% of the third $1 million
  - 2% of the fourth $1 million
  - And so forth, with a 1% charge on everything above $4 million

Today, the original Lehman formula is no longer sustainable, due to the inflationary effects since it was first introduced more than 40 years ago. Today, the Double Lehman Formula is more popular, in which each percentage is doubled. In the last 18-24 months or so, I've seen a few instances of the Triple Lehman Formula (or hybrid versions closely resembling this), meaning a revised Lehman Formula as below (reflecting both the Double and Triple Lehman variations):

Double Lehman Formula:	Triple Lehman Formula
• 10% for the first $1 million	• 15% for the first $1 million
• 8% for the second $1 million	• 12% for the second $1 million
• 6% for the third $1 million	• 9% for the third $1 million
• 4% for the fourth $1 million	• 8% for the fourth $1 million
• 2% on all amounts thereafter	• 4% on all amounts thereafter

Notwithstanding the above, people often ask what a reasonable success fee percentage would be for their particular deal. Although it's complicated to answer this question without certain details, on the following page is a general summary of what reasonable success fees would be from qualified advisory firms executing a comprehensive and global sell-side strategy, expressed as a percentage of the transaction value

COVERAGE

As the seller of a company, you face a variety of possible outcomes. As discussions with potential investors unfold, you may be surprised at the variation in the expressions of interest received, ranging from investors seeking strategic partnerships to joint ventures, licensing deals to reverse takeover structures. Until you are in the marketplace, speaking with investors and determining their level of interest and how they view the opportunity, you cannot predict how they will respond—or the type of deal structure you may ultimately agree to in your transaction. Subsequently, it's imperative that the scope of services provided and the spectrum of covered transactions are well defined for the benefit of both seller and advisor.

TERM

The term of the agreement specifies how long the engagement—and therefore the associated exclusivity—lasts. Engagement letters define the term and usually include a clause for automatic renewal on a monthly or quarterly basis until the sales process has been completed, providing that neither party terminates the agreement. A six- to 12-month term is typical since that's commonly how long a sales process takes from start to finish. It's worth paying attention to termination clauses in your agreement with your advisor. Deciding to terminate an agreement and then noticing that you've agreed to an onerous and costly termination clause can be an unpleasant experience to say the least.

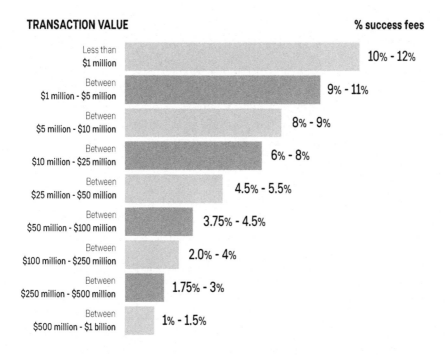

TRANSACTION VALUE   **% success fees**

Less than $1 million	10% - 12%
Between $1 million - $5 million	9% - 11%
Between $5 million - $10 million	8% - 9%
Between $10 million - $25 million	6% - 8%
Between $25 million - $50 million	4.5% - 5.5%
Between $50 million - $100 million	3.75% - 4.5%
Between $100 million - $250 million	2.0% - 4%
Between $250 million - $500 million	1.75% - 3%
Between $500 million - $1 billion	1% - 1.5%

TRAILER CLAUSE OR TAIL PERIOD

A trailer clause, or tail, is a period of time after the termination of the agreement between the seller and the advisor during which the advisor will still be compensated if a transaction closes. Trailer clauses can vary in length but usually range from 12 to 36 months, with the average period being closer to 24 months.

The advisor will ask for a trailer clause to remove any incentive that could leave the advisor shortchanged. It's easy to imagine a situation in which an advisor brings a buyer to the table, after which an unscrupulous seller could fire the advisor, close the deal himself, and avoid paying a success fee. Trailer clauses prevent this scenario and are common in M&A mandates.

There are other, less nefarious reasons why a trailer or tail period clause is a good idea. Transactions can be, and are, suspended or delayed for an array of reasons (death of a family member, illnesses, change in leadership structure within acquiring company, commencement of a summer or other holiday period, downturn in the seller's business due to unforeseen changes, and so on), and are also contingent upon the participation of several stakeholders. During this suspension, an advisor's term of engagement may expire. Within the bounds of a reasonable timeframe, your advisor would have a justifiable argument for compensation if they introduced the buyer to you but the successful transaction was delayed for reasons outside of the advisor's influence.

A NOTE ON TERMS OF ENGAGEMENT

Getting the right agreement in place with an M&A advisor is an important factor for most sellers. If you'd benefit from speaking with someone who can provide an external perspective on the terms being proposed to you, feel free to reach out to us at *ExitSupport@markcarmichael.com* to discuss.

EXPENSES

Advisors typically will seek reimbursement for out-of-pocket expenses incurred during the engagement period as they relate to travel, research, and marketing material preparation (graphic design/layout of marketing documents, etc.). It is not uncommon, therefore, for engagement letters to state that the client will cover any such reasonable expenses incurred by the advisor in the performance of its services. That said, it's in your interest to ensure that such provisions in the letter of engagement enable you to exercise certain controls as to the limits of such expenses.

Clients often impose a maximum limit for out-of-pocket expenses, either in a given calendar month, or a set limit for any expense not to exceed $X without the client's written consent. It is also in your interest to stipulate that expenses be claimed monthly, thereby avoiding the accrual of expenses over a number of months, which can equate to a nasty surprise.

TERMINATION

Your engagement letter should explicitly state the rights of termination by either party both during and after the initial term of mandate. Most agreements are written to automatically renew on a monthly basis until canceled, in writing, by either you or the banker.

* * *

The sale of your business will be an emotional roller coaster at times, and a lot of work. You may develop deal fatigue if the process drags on. Buyers are going to ask difficult questions, potentially disagree with your views, and challenge your assumptions.

Your advisor should be someone you will enjoy working with, whose opinion you respect, whose integrity is unquestioned and who has the team, resources, commitment, and energy to endure the process and time required to reach a successful result. If you focus on the above questions, you improve your chances of choosing the right advisor to sell your company.

CHAPTER 5

FORMING YOUR DEAL TEAM

"Know what you're doing, love what you're doing, believe in what you're doing and surround yourself with the right people."

—Will Rogers

Imagine negotiating a deal in which your own attorney is so arrogant and inept that the other side's attorney has to coach him on what to do. I saw precisely that happen—in fact, I was the one who asked the opposing attorney for help. If I hadn't, the deal never would have closed.

Our client was selling a growing and profitable online business. We had to do some heavy lifting to get the accounting in order, but buyers were interested and soon we were in the advanced stages of the deal, drafting the definitive sales agreement. At this point, I knew that we had a problem. My client had insisted on retaining his long-term lawyer (a family member on his wife's side), who was a competent attorney in other respects, but had no experience in transactional law. He simply didn't know what he was doing and was weak in negotiating the deal points of the agreements with the buyer's lawyers. He was arrogant, too. At several key points in the negotiation, he refused our guidance. The deal nearly collapsed. And nearly collapsed again. And again.

Fortunately, we had developed a strong relationship with the buyer's lawyer. I reached out to him, explained the seller's lawyer's limitations, and asked for help. In exchange, I promised we would do all we could to minimize the brain damage for the buyer's lawyer as we struggled through. He was sympathetic to our lawyer and helped him along. Despite the fact that the deal almost collapsed *seven* times because our client's attorney kept creating obstacle after obstacle, we eventually closed.

Getting the right team around you is fundamental to your success in selling your company. The deal team is the single most manageable component in determining whether a company will sell. As with any team, the quality of the players determines a very large part in the overall success of the team. Get it right and your probability of a successful close increases considerably. Get it wrong and a successful transaction becomes much more elusive.

Yet many business owners do, in fact, fail to build the team most likely to achieve success. They assemble a mediocre team that delivers a disappointing result—one that fails to meet the owner's expectations, or fails to close a deal at all. The sad part is that with even a basic understanding of the importance of having the right team, the owner can mitigate the probability of an undesirable result by establishing the right team around him/her.

Failure in this respect happens for many reasons. In the previous chapter I discussed how to select your team captain—your M&A advisor. Now let's go through the remaining team members.

Key members of a typical deal team are:

- 1-2 trusted senior management team members
- M&A advisor/investment banker
- Transaction/deal attorney
- CPA/accountant
- The tax attorney
- Financial/wealth advisor

You may not have an ongoing relationship with an investment banker or M&A advisor. On the other hand, you probably do have a relationship with an accountant and a lawyer. But just because you've worked with your CPA/CA for 20 years, or your lawyer has handled all your IP protection and commercial leases, does not automatically qualify these individuals or their firms to be on the team that sells your company. This is the first pitfall—going with whom you know, rather than the best for the job. You must vet your team members carefully, seeking specific skills and experience, to maximize the likelihood of a great outcome. Just as in sports, if you don't have the right team together before the season starts, it's not difficult to predict where you'll be at the end of the season. You're the coach; it's your job—and in your best interests—to put the right team together to ensure victory.

Expect the sales process to require six to nine months, often longer, seldom shorter. It needs to accomplish two things that can work at cross purposes: (1) prepare the business for sale and conduct an exhaustive exit process, and (2) keep everybody focused on running the business.

The sales process moves through these stages:

- Education & Strategy: Preparing you and your business
- Preparation of marketing materials
- Investor outreach
- Initial buyer due diligence and expressions of interest
- Meetings
- Negotiations
- Closing

Too often, successful business owners leap into the process of selling the company without sufficient advance thought or preparation. It's as if, now that they've decided to sell, they can't wait to get it done. By build-

Key Deal Team Tasks	Why It's Important to You
Identifying and researching a global pool of strategic and financial investors, and identifying 2-3 appropriate contacts (and details) for each targeted investor.	Failure to create a highly targeted investor list leads to lacklustre results, including reduced potential for competitive bidding, and an overall successful result for your exit.
Engaging and establishing meaningful dialogues with each target investor.	Every transaction comes down to people dealing with people. It makes sense to establish positive, trust-based dialogues with each investor wherever possible.
Negotiating highest valuation and deal terms.	Inexperienced negotiators produce suboptimal deal terms. Informed sellers know: first, establish competitive bidding; then leverage this, along with positive investor dialogues to arrive at the best deals.
Drafting definitive agreements.	As with negotiating, you'll want to have representatives at the table who have done this many times and can show you their expertise.
Obtaining appropriate advice on the sale of your business.	Reliable accounting advice on M&A deals requires a different skill set than what your regular accountant or CPA may possess.
Developing professional, compelling, and concise marketing documents.	You want to disclose the right amount of information—neither too little nor too much—to intrigue your targets and precipitate further conversation.
Providing you with regular updates on investor communications	Be sure you have a designated lead on the team who is responsible for this, as you're busy running your company.
Coaching you on investor calls and communications.	How you say something can be as important as what you say.
Engaging investors in sophisticated debates over valuation to effectively challenge investor valuations and propose advantageous deal structures.	Serious buyers will bring big guns to the table. Is your team able to match them?
Developing trust-based relationships with investors to ensure ongoing negotiations remain on track, positive, and moving toward closing.	Mutual respect, integrity, and personal relationships are the foundation of effective negotiations and prerequisites to getting a deal done.
Creating a competitive bidding environment.	Always the surest way to get the best deal.

ing your team the right way—and by understanding the "rules" of selling businesses before you embark upon your exit journey—you increase the chance of celebrating a successful transaction, potentially shorten the timeframe to closing, and minimize the stress, financial costs, and odds of a deal falling over in the advanced stages. Build a team in which you have deep confidence and you will breathe more easily, knowing your company will be presented in the best light, that everyone will act and present themselves profes- sionally at all times, and that communications between team members are aligned, coordinated, and effective.

Your deal team will handle many, many questions and issues. On page 110, you'll find an overview of key tasks you should expect your deal team to assume, along with a brief explanation as to why each is of importance to you.

WHAT DO I TELL MY EMPLOYEES?

In the late 1990s, a public company approached me about buying a technology firm I had started. I entered into negotiations, and once we had a Letter of Intent I was quite open with my employees about what was going on.

I wouldn't do that again.

Although I was to remain with the company after it was sold, I discovered that my announcement had created a great deal of stress on my team during the ensuing months. One employee later admitted to me that she began seeking a new job as soon as she learned of my plans, because she (thought she) knew I wouldn't be fully in control and couldn't look out for her anymore. The levels of anxiety varied, but the bottom line is people fear the unknown—unknown leadership, unknown future, unknown changes.

These fears are not unfounded. New owners often cut jobs in search of efficiencies, and they bring with them a new workplace culture. Even before that happens though, as the seller, you face another consideration: it isn't sold until it's sold. Deals fall through for all kinds of reasons. Until you arrive at closing day—and the money is in your account—you run the risk of adding stress and uncertainty to your team's lives that may not be warranted. And if word gets out to customers or competitors that a sale is in the works, that's rarely to your or your buyer's benefit.

On the other hand, it doesn't feel good to give the wrong impression, much less lie, to people you rely on and who rely on you. The solution for most entrepreneurs is, when asked, to provide a truthful explanation by advising that you are exploring a strategic relationship with another company. After all, more than one of our clients have set out to sell their business and in the end, found themselves in a joint venture arrangement with an investor that brought cash and commercial synergies that reignited our client's passions to grow the company to new levels under this strategic relationship. The best advice: think carefully about how you will explain the situation long before you are asked the question.

All that said, you won't get your deal done without the help of key, trusted employees. They need to be in the know, and they may be quite excited about the sale. Often, an acquisition means growth opportunities for them, so it doesn't hurt to let them in on your plans. A cautionary note: they must understand and respect how important it is not to discuss the plans with other employees—and not everyone does. I've seen several instances where the business owner has chosen individuals he thought he could entrust with the confidential task of preparing to sell the company, only to find that word soon spread among employees, resulting in insecurity, and even anger.

SELECTING THE RIGHT DEAL ATTORNEY

Legal matters lie at the center of an M&A deal, so having the right transaction lawyer is a critical necessity to both seller and buyer. In the same way that each party has an M&A advisor, so too will each side have its own lawyer. Your legal representative's ability to communicate (and negotiate) effectively and efficiently can make the difference between a successful deal concluded and a deal gone horribly wrong.

Don't make the mistake here of being inappropriately loyal. You may have worked with your attorney for years, but that is not a reason to put him on your deal team if they don't have the necessary experience and skills in M&A transactions. In an M&A transaction, the lawyers for both sides work together to draft terms of the sale and purchase agreement. These agreements are typically lengthy, complex, and employ obscure terminology that seems intended to intimidate those of us who did not attend law school.

Nevertheless, qualified, capable, and experienced transaction lawyers are most often pleasant to deal with. Yet many buyers and sellers often don't hire a qualified, capable and experienced transaction lawyer—and that's when the problems arise. So how do you determine if a lawyer belongs on the team?

The simple answer: ask the right questions to develop an understanding as to whether they're the right party or not. Here's a list to get you started:

- How much experience does the firm or lawyer have?
- Are they experienced in drafting and negotiating complex transaction agreements?
- Can they provide case studies or otherwise of M&A work completed on behalf of recent clients?
- Will they focus on getting *any* deal done or the *right* deal done?
- Can they give you an estimate or range of expected fees? Will they offer you a fixed fee? Will they offer to cap their fees? An inability to provide an estimate of fees may indicate inexperience.
- Do you feel that the lawyer would represent you well in the eyes of the purchaser?
- How emotional is the lawyer? Will they help you keep your cool during negotiations? How experienced a negotiator are they?
- Are the partners who pitched you going to be the partners working on your deal or will they allocate this to an associate or another junior team member?
- How do they intend to keep you informed throughout the process? Ensure that they don't keep you in the dark. This is your deal.
- What assurances can they provide that they won't "over-lawyer" the deal to rack up billable hours?
- Do you feel they will prioritize the issues at hand?
- How responsive will they be during the process?

Lawyers become key players during the final stages of a deal.

Hiring the right deal lawyer is vital to getting your deal across the line. At my firm, if the client insists on utilizing the services of a law firm that does not possess the appropriate experience in M&A transactions, we will not engage with that client. In 2020, we had a European client who was adamant on using a lifelong lawyer friend of his who had provided general commercial legal advice to his company for some time. After speaking directly with this lawyer, I had no confidence in his ability regarding the sale of the business. I suggested to the seller that he use a qualified firm instead and upon closing on the sale of his business, that he pay his lawyer friend a €50,000 "loyalty bonus" for his years of service. He rejected this advice and we declined the opportunity to sell his business.

SELECTING THE RIGHT ACCOUNTANT

Your accountant will be involved with many aspects of the deal. Their first job—and one that your present accountant certainly can tackle—will be producing financial statements that are current and ready for review by your deal team. Solid financial statements properly report the business to a buyer. Depending on the size of your company, audited financial statements may not necessarily be required, but investors typically prefer to see reviewed-level financial statements before proceeding to advanced stages of due diligence. The task of getting financial information in order is often the major cause of delays preventing us from bringing a company to market in a timely manner. Complete financial reporting is an important part of your exit planning; because it can take a while, start now if you haven't already.

SELECTING A FINANCIAL/WEALTH ADVISOR

This may seem premature, but you'll do well to plan ahead. Depending on the value you realize when you sell your business, your wealth status is going to change. Many owners receive a life-changing amount of money.

Those funds are the tool to help you realize your life's wishes. You're going to need a financial advisor who understands the unique challenges of your own personal situation and who can manage your wealth and planning for the future.

Many clients are surprised when we advise them that they are about to become a "high-net-worth individual" (HNWI). The financial services industry assigns this label to individuals whose investable assets exceed a defined threshold, typically north of $1 million, excluding their primary residence. If you're going to have more than $5 million to invest, you're considered "very-high-net-worth." And some of you reading this may soon enter the world of "ultra-high-net-worth status": $30 million or more in liquid financial assets.

Finally, if you'll have less than $1 million out of the transaction, but more than $100,000, you're considered "affluent" by people who manage money. Regardless of the label a wealth advisor might put on you, one thing is certain, in order to achieve your goals now and for future generations, you will require a robust blend of tax planning and financial advisory services.

Here are some of the considerations you may face before, during and after a successful exit.

INCOME TAX PLANNING AND COMPLIANCE

Irrespective of where you live, today's ever-changing tax environment requires a strategic approach and a range of strategies to handle the proceeds of the sale of your business efficiently. Issues that will potentially be more important for you during and after the sale of your business include:

- Annual tax returns
- Domestic and international reporting requirements/obligations
- Tax payments

- Tax authority communications
- Interface with your advisor

INVESTMENT PLANNING

Your investment strategy should be balanced, while offering you the flexibility you need to capitalize on new opportunities as they emerge. You may find yourself concerned with:

- Tax-efficient investing
- Reporting and disclosures
- Structure of domestic and foreign holdings and asset allocation
- Selection of investment holding vehicle and domicile
- An independent, third-party sounding board

ESTATE, TRUST AND GIFT PLANNING, AND COMPLIANCE

In the absence of appropriate planning, estate and inheritance taxes can considerably affect the wealth available for future generations. Your plans should be reviewed regularly to address changes in tax laws and in your personal situation. You may need help with:

- Tax reporting and disclosures
- Consulting regarding foreign local jurisdiction laws and customs
- Lifetime giving to family and charities
- Effective use of trusts and other entities
- Desire to establish a foundation
- Assessing and coordinating estate documentation, arrangements, and related matters

PHILANTHROPY

Many entrepreneurs are interested in the way philanthropy can allow them to use some of the proceeds of the sale in a way that benefits others. An ideal philanthropic giving strategy achieves the family's charitable goals while being tax efficient. Topics of interest include:

- Utilizing charitable trusts and foundations in wealth planning
- Assisting in financial and social responsibility
- Establishing the time horizon for giving
- Managing philanthropic goals and estate planning
- Evaluating tax efficiency of current and proposed giving

INSURANCE AND RISK MANAGEMENT

Increased wealth means rethinking how to protect your family's well-being and assets from various risks. This means obtaining suitable insurance coverage and making tactical choices about forms of asset ownership. You may want advice regarding:

- Policy comparisons
- Analyzing assets and beneficial ownership structures
- Independent and objective assessment of life insurance coverage
- Insurance for liability and investment purposes

FAMILY OFFICES

For ultra-high-net-worth families, the administrative and managerial needs can be extensive. A family office—effectively a staff to manage your money, charitable giving, and other financial matters—can be an effective solution. You'll want to think about:

- Tax considerations
- Family office regulation
- Day-to-day operations
- Structure and creation (for example, single-family offices versus multiple-family offices)

LIFESTYLE INVESTMENTS

Ownership of yachts, airplanes, classic automobiles, watch collections, wine collections, and art brings unique tax challenges. In the interest of tax-efficient ownership of these types of assets, you'll want to think about:

• Support planning for acquisitions and/or dispositions
• Choice of entity/jurisdiction where the asset is to be owned
• Domestic and international tax considerations
• VAT compliance and planning
• Facilitate assessment of assets

THE CEO

Remember that list of team members at the top of the chapter? The CEO—that's (likely) you—is the team coach. Your M&A advisor captains your team and will, at numerous times, lead the process.

You'll have a critical role to play in strategic conversations with investors. Your advisor should always set up and lead these conversations. (It looks amateurish for an owner to try to sell his own business.) Your M&A advisor will brief you, set up calls and meetings, and keep things flowing during the conversation. He should fully prepare you around what to say (or not—timing of conversations matters) and how to say it—for example, how to address questions accurately and with conviction.

My team and I always advise owners to be themselves, to be prepared to address challenging questions. If an investor asks, "Industry standard for growth has been 20% in the past year, but you only posted 11% growth. Why?" you'll want to be ready for that question and be able to explain the reason and how you're addressing the situation.

Finally, be likeable, always be honest, and let the investor see who you are. Your passion and conviction are what built the business, and they will help sell it.

Getting your team right is critical. It may be the most important thing you do as an owner preparing to sell a business. "Right" comes down to asking the correct questions and listening carefully to the answers. Take your time. Be thoughtful. Consider carefully whose advice you accept. With the proper players in place and a clear strategy defined through your exit plan, you're ready to begin the process of selling your company in earnest.

CHAPTER 6

PRE-MARKETING AND PRE-SALES

*"You were born to win, but to be a winner,
you must plan to win, prepare to win, and expect to win."*

—Zig Ziglar

A few years ago, while on honeymoon in the Sabi Sand Reserve in South Africa, I met a fellow safari enthusiast, a German steel pipe manufacturer. Over dinner one night, he recounted how a few years back he received a call from an M&A advisor who wanted to pitch a business acquisition to him. The advisor offered to send over the information memorandum (IM), and the pipe maker agreed to take a look at it.

Later that day, a comprehensive PDF document arrived in his in-box. It was more than 50 pages of dense text describing another German steel fabricating firm that was an indirect competitor of his. He perused the document but there were almost no graphs or charts to show key facts quickly. He was going to have to read the entire thing, and he didn't have time—or patience, I imagine. But then something caught his eye, he told me.

Toward the back was a list of the firm's top customers, including details about their contracts. Now *this* was interesting, so he began to read carefully. He had no intention of acquiring his competitor's business but was grateful to have received very important trade secrets.

Over the next four months or so, he boasted that he was able to secure the business of two of his competitor's top clients, thanks to the information he found inside that IM.

When all was said and done, the owner who had been trying to sell failed to reach his goal (in part, I suspect, because his advisor only marketed his firm within Germany, it seemed), and was in a worse position than when he started the sales process, having lost money and clients.

The fault here lay with the M&A advisor, who obviously provided bad advice during the pre-marketing phase of the sales process about what should be included in the IM and to whom it should be sent, and then compounded that error by marketing the company to a relatively small pool of potential buyers.

I share this story here because it is a stark illustration of the importance of knowing how to appropriately prepare for the marketing of your business and further, understanding how to control what information goes to whom, and when. This process is central to the marketing and pre-marketing of your business.

In this chapter, we'll visit the four major pre-marketing steps that lay the groundwork for the marketing stage (also referred to as the investor outreach stage):

- Marketing materials development
- Investor research
- Confidentiality agreements
- Professional presentation

As you proceed through the pre-marketing process and create your marketing materials, you are creating layers of information that you will deploy in a strategic choreography to attract, engage with, educate and ultimately conclude a transaction with your best global investor. All of the players on your team—both internal managers and external advisors—must pull in the same direction and reinforce the same messages. Conflicting signals compromise credibility and effectiveness by creating confusion and doubt.

Your objective is to be able to provide key factual information for a potential buyer that portrays the investment opportunity in its most favorable light. Trust and momentum depend on the deal team's ability to anticipate investor questions and have convincing responses prepared. All communications (in person, phone, e-mail, marketing materials) must paint a clear and consistent picture of market growth and opportunity and relate it to your company's projections. All communications must articulate underlying assumptions and value drivers and outline how these opportunities will be captured. Once again, your advisor should oversee this process and lead those involved through this process.

Finally, as the owner you must stand at the nexus throughout the process, keeping the company focused, creating the correct management incentives and support, managing the advisory team, and navigating the course between running an effective business and steering it toward a successful sale.

A good advisor will manage this process effectively. For instance, there are subtle ways to create a sense of scarcity on the part of buyers by displaying the uniqueness of the investment opportunity to suitors. The advisor can cultivate a controlled sense of urgency, stressing the options available to the seller and the opportunity at hand for the buyer. Value cannot be maximized in a vacuum: the advisor has to understand the courting party's agenda, value drivers (think synergies within your business that they find most attractive), and deal-making and deal-breaking issues. All in all, the objective is to keep value high and avoid the deal fatigue that results from a drawn-out process.

By this point in the book, you know that I'm going to tell you that early preparation is a key to success. Start the work described in this chapter as soon as you are ready—give yourself time to get things right.

Let's take a look at the teaser, confidential information memorandum, and supplemental presentation documents in the order you'll present them.

YOUR MARKETING GAME PLAN

A simplified version of your game plan looks like this:

- Your advisor creates the Confidential Information Memorandum (CIM or IM), the teaser, and any supplemental presentation documents.

- After exhaustively researching and developing a global pool of highly targeted potential investors, the advisor initiates contact to present the teaser.

- Those investors who express initial interest are required to en- ter into a confidentiality agreement, after which they are pre- sented with the IM.

- This leads to further discussions with interested parties, and the advisor deploys the supplemental marketing documents as appropriate to enrich the dialogue and deepen their understanding of—and attraction toward—the seller's business.

- The objective of the marketing materials is to educate and heighten investor interest, leading to ever-advancing—and deepening—discussions that will ultimately define the best owner for your business and lead to a successful transaction.

This is a comprehensive, time-consuming, and delicate process, easily derailed by missteps if your advisor doesn't know what he or she is doing.

MARKETING MATERIALS DEVELOPMENT

THE TEASER

Although it is the first thing you send to potential investors, the teaser should not be the first thing the advisor creates. It is typically a one- to two-page (on rare occasions as long as five pages, but relevance and brevity are usually the norm) document distilled from the much longer Information Memorandum. It has one objective: to cause the recipient to respond positively, seeking more information. The teaser's objective is to create an enticing overview of the opportunity, while deliberately omitting enough information to enable the recipient to identify the company. To conceal a company's identity, we'll often add elements of ambiguity around items such as the location (for example "Southeastern US" instead of "Tampa"). Or, we may include the city name, but refer to it as an automotive parts manufacturer instead of the more detailed description of automotive glass manufacturing.

Nevertheless, many teasers fail at this most basic task. Review 100 random teasers produced by 100 different advisors and you will likely find that at least 50% of them have missed the mark. Teasers are not just text; they are (or at least, *should be*) artfully designed, eye-catching documents created to generate interest and convey credibility.

After reading the teaser, the buyer must have a clear understanding of the company and the nature of the opportunity. The teaser must contain enough information to stimulate the buyer to want to learn more, yet not so much information that the identity of your business can be reverse-engineered by reading it. Owners often don't want to publicize the fact that they are for sale, as rumors to that effect are liable to disrupt customer and supplier relations, upset employees, or give competitors an advantage. Potential buyers, on the other hand, will not want to go through the time and effort of executing an NDA (which would most likely require review by the corporate counsel, etc.) without a sufficient high-level understanding of what the opportunity is and why it is appropriate for his firm.

A teaser should include this basic information:

- When the company was founded;
- How the firm generates revenue;
- Sales and revenue mix of the company's products/services;
- How its products/services are sold and distributed;
- Summary of financial performance for last three years, including projected revenues for the next 12 to 24 months;
- Into which markets, industries, and geographies the firm sells;
- Rationale for the transaction;
- Where its offices are located; and
- A summary of investment highlights that portray the differentiators and strengths of your firm (such as intellectual property, long-term blue-chip clients, or an impressive annual revenue growth rate).

What many teasers fail to include is "the ask." That is, they fail to clearly state the goals of the proposed transaction. Why, in other words, did you send a prospect this e-mail? Do you want to sell 100% of the company? Are you looking for growth capital? Is your goal a partial sale of the equity (i.e., a minority or majority position)? Or are you seeking a strategic partner who can assist you in taking the company to the next level? The absence of such information in teasers seems like a forehead slapper, but you might be surprised by what we've seen—or rather, *not* seen—in teasers.

THE INFORMATION MEMORANDUM

The Information Memorandum (IM) is also referred to as the Confidential Information Memorandum, the "offering memorandum," or simply "the book." It is the initial, detailed summary of your business that investors will use to determine whether or not this opportunity warrants further investigation. In other words, it's an important document. The IM should sufficiently address the investor's need for more information but leave the reader with plenty of questions, encouraging a meaningful follow-up discussion between your advisor and the potential investor. The IM likely will be distributed by the investor internally and, depending on the size of the buyer's company, is likely to end up on the desks of the CEO and board members. This is an opportunity to put your best foot forward, ensuring that the document includes a well-defined opportunity, logically and compellingly presented, highlighting the areas of strategic synergy, any unrealized potential, and other investment highlights.

However, despite what many websites, blogs and advisors may tell you, an IM is not the thing that will sell your company, and as I mentioned earlier, it should not be designed to do so. It should be written with the objective of sufficiently intriguing the reader to ask for more information.

Like it or not, nobody is going to find your IM so compelling that they will sit down and read a text-heavy, overly lengthy document. Not at first, anyway. What they want to know is whether or not, on first glance, there may be a fit between your firm and theirs.

Although the disclosure of sensitive information does become necessary as the sales process advances, releasing it too early is unnecessary and potentially dangerous, as the person reading it may also be one of your competitors. While they no doubt will be very interested in your company's playbook, there is little or no benefit to you in them having it. Detailed information should be disclosed to each prospective investor once they have sufficiently advanced through the process to build trust with you, and your advisor has verified them as a genuine and financially capable acquirer.

To compile the IM, your advisor will submit an information request to you as you begin work together. The information request will encompass your financials, products/services, geographic footprint, any legal matters outstanding (ongoing lawsuits with suppliers, customers, employees, ex-employees, etc.), the sector/market in which you operate, forecasts, and so on. This information allows the advisor to better understand your company and forms the basis of the IM.

As this step is likely to be the first exchange between you and your advisor of confidential and sensitive information, ensure that the appropriate pro- tective measures are in place. Advisors will have a standard non-disclosure agreement (NDA)— also referred to as a Confidentiality Agreement (CA)—that they will send you (if matters of confidentiality have not already been addressed in your agreement with them) that will protect the exchange of information between you and them. You'll also need an NDA with prospective buyers.

NON-DISCLOSURE OR CONFIDENTIALITY AGREEMENTS

One of the first steps your advisor must take with an interested buyer is securing an NDA or CA. Be sure that this agreement is in place before even the name of your business is disclosed. You will be exchanging confidential information, and more of it as the conversation progresses. Generally speaking, in the absence of an NDA, buyers and sellers do not have any obligation to keep the other's information confidential. If there is no NDA in place between the parties, recipients may be free to use the confidential information they receive as they see fit, even if that use is damaging to you.

By executing a properly constructed NDA, both parties may proceed in confidence.

A good NDA should include clauses that:

- Forbid potential buyers from disclosing even the fact that your business is for sale, as well as information regarding your business.

- Forbid buyers from using confidential information for any other purpose than evaluating the business for sale.

- Forbid poaching of employees. Some buyers resist this clause, particularly if they compete in your industry. A good compromise can be a modification that allows for general, non-specific solicitations made through online or print media.

- List what is considered confidential information.

- Oblige the buyer to acknowledge that this information has competitive value.

- Include a covenant that the seller does not warrant completeness or accuracy of the information, and that it is incumbent upon the recipient to conduct due diligence.

Plan your disclosures. Increasingly sensitive information should be released later in the due diligence process. For example, I often field requests from buyers early in the process for a detailed list of the seller's clients. Rather than provide identifying information, we'll anonymize the customer data, removing specific details that would allow the buyer to identify the customer, or any other data that could be harmful to our client if disclosed (such as individual customer pricing details). We want to share information effectively, but also avoid regrets about sharing too much too soon with a potential buyer who then walked away with a lot of the seller's secrets in his pocket.

Your advisor typically will negotiate any changes to the NDA/CA with potential investors, minimizing the time you need to spend on this part of the process. NDA/CAs are usually agreed upon with the seller in a reasonably short timeframe. However, this step can become a tedious and protracted one if the other party has multiple changes or objections that lead to marked-up versions going back and forth. It's not uncommon for an overzealous lawyer (often a new addition to the firm) to try to demonstrate his or her value by making a project out of what should be a straightforward exercise. In any event, the burden of securing the signed NDAs should fall on the shoulders of your advisor, saving you time and legal fees.

Finally, pay attention to how your potential buyer negotiates the NDA. This is a relatively short document, likely to run to 1,000 words or so. The way the buyer approaches putting the NDA in place and agreeing to its terms can often tell you a lot about how they will negotiate during the rest of the process. If the buyer is rubbing you the wrong way at this early stage, you might think about finding another buyer.

SUPPLEMENTAL DOCUMENTS

Supplemental documents are follow-on materials that serve several purposes. They can inform investors about specific aspects of the seller's business worth highlighting—for example, specific synergies between the seller and buyer, or a brief summary of the seller's IP, an overview of a recent advertising campaign, a financial report about a new market, or a trailing 12-month financial summary.

These documents give the advisor an opportunity to further build a dialogue with the investor, sharing information while also learning about that investor. Investors may be looking at more than one deal; supplemental documents help earn and maintain foremost position in the investor's mind. The more your advisor can learn about the investor, the more relevant information he can send, the better.

THINK LIKE YOUR BUYER

What is your buyer going to want to know in order to become interested and remain interested? Once again, take a walk in his shoes. Now is the moment to invest time and energy to tell your story, because that's ultimately what you are doing with the financials, projections, and narrative about your company that make up the IM. These materials tell the investor a story—a story he or she may choose to step into and complete.

Financials, of course, are central to that story. In Chapter 2, I discussed the importance of externally audited financial statements and normalized EBITDA reporting. The act of producing these documents often is the bulk of the work you must do to assist your advisor in preparing the IM. It's worth noting that while business owners typically prepare their financial statements for tax purposes, these are not necessarily ideal for purposes of selling your business. Disclosing tax statements too early during the sale process can be a costly mistake, as they typically fail to depict the true earnings capability of a business.

So what is your investor going to want to know? If you are seeking a strategic buyer, focus on identifying and highlighting potential synergies, such as your geographic focus, exclusive distribution rights, intellectual property, client profiles, details of long-term customer contracts, and so on. If your goal is a financial buyer, be sure you paint a clear picture of your cash flow and have carefully normalized your EBITDA. A word of caution here: as I noted in Chapter 2, you may be tempted to aggressively normalize EBITDA in order to show the best earnings scenario. Remember, though, that a diligent buyer will investigate this area carefully. If you are too aggressive on this front, you run the risk of eroding trust between you and buyer, making him or her skittish. Mutual trust is fundamental to completing the optimal deal.

131

READY, SET—REASSESS

Momentum is a powerful thing, and you likely have a lot of it at this point. Nevertheless, now is an excellent time to pick up your head and look around. Although you're doing the work you must to put your best foot forward, consider the state of the field you are about to walk onto. In other words, is this the right time to sell?

Take a hard look at the business cycle you operate in and the current economic conditions. Has the market outlook changed since you began working toward a sale? Have interest rates gone up, and how will that affect what buyers can offer you? Is your industry in a down-cycle that may depress valuation? Bottom line: in light of current conditions, is it still the right time to sell?

PROFESSIONAL PRESENTATION

As I noted above, trust is essential to getting a deal done. One of the easiest ways to erode trust and confidence is by being sloppy or simply unprofessional. If you receive a cover letter with your name misspelled, or look at a resume that includes a typographical error or feels like it was designed in 1993, what is your response? You're probably skeptical, if not downright dismissive.

We all know that first impressions matter. Beginning with the teaser and accompanying e-mail, your advisor should put your best foot forward. Your documents should be professionally designed and carefully written and proofread. Such materials project sincerity and trustworthiness, while a poorly produced document achieves exactly the opposite effect. In our firm, we triple-check every document going out the door. That doesn't mean I read everything three times; rather, three different individuals look for typos, grammatical correctness, consistency, and overall tone and flow. Anyone who is proofreading is empowered to challenge the authors openly and propose revisions. Often a debate ensues, but in the end we have a thoroughly checked, professionally produced, aesthetically pleasing document that articulates the hard facts, avoids exaggerations and alleged "marketing" nonsense like "once in a lifetime opportunity," "future-proof technology" or "act now." Our teasers are almost always two pages or shorter; some buyers review dozens of opportunities per month, so we know our job is to attract their attention—period.

You are, in effect, getting ready for a first date. So dress up, stand tall, be intriguing, demonstrate an understanding of your potential partner, and show them something to make them want more.

CHAPTER 7

GO TO MARKET: MARKETING AND SELLING

"Opportunity dances with those who are on the dance floor."

—H. Jackson Brown, Jr.

I received a call one day from the managing director of a large and growing call center with operations in the UK and Manila. He was in a bind, and frustrated. He wanted to sell his business, and family issues obliged him to sell it quickly. His firm had been growing fast and he had recently signed up several long-term contracts with blue-chip corporate clients. The company had recurring revenue, an impressive list of clients, and a proven management team. He knew that if he waited two years he could earn substantially more in a sale, but family issues took priority.

He had hired another M&A firm and paid them a monthly retainer for six months, but they had failed to generate a single lead. There was, apparently, zero interest from buyers. The owner fired the advisors and, on the recommendation of a mutual acquaintance, called me.

This result didn't make sense, because he had a good company built on recurring revenues, showing continued growth, and a strong and growing EBITDA. He explained all of this to me during the course of a 45-minute conversation. At the end of the call we agreed to sign an NDA so I could look more deeply into his company and make a recommendation. He sent me a packet of information that included a copy of the agreement he had with the previous advisor.

My heart sank when I read it. Clearly, the owner had not asked his attorney to review that contract. He had agreed that for a period of three years following the termination of his engagement, should the company be sold to *any* party, whether that party had been contacted by the previous advisor or not, they would pay the former advisor 7.5% of the transaction value. I felt awful for this guy. He clearly had hired the wrong advisor, who then underperformed magnificently by failing to effectively market or sell the company—and hamstrung the owner by essentially forbidding him to sell the business for three years.

That success fee could have been tolerable if the original M&A advisor actually had done his job. When he didn't, it became a poison pill. Buyer beware: know exactly what your advisor's strategy is to market your business and how qualified and effective they are in carrying out this exercise.

Get out on the dance floor.

Marketing and selling your business is where your M&A advisor really earns his or her fee. I've made this point repeatedly, but I'll make it again. Your objective, and thus your advisor's objective, should be to create a competitive bidding process involving international qualified buyers. That situation creates the environment for you to sell to your best buyer and to realize the goals you identified in your exit plan. The job of bringing that situation about is primarily your advisor's responsibility, which means he or she must know how to market and sell your company, and do so effectively. Be mindful of the quote at the beginning of this chapter; it will be the effectiveness of your marketing and sales strategy that will determine if your dance card is full or empty.

If you've read this far, such a statement seems self-evident. Yet there are plenty of advisors (in my experience, most) who simply don't do this well. They don't see themselves as being in the marketing business and they don't embody an entrepreneurial mind-set that is focused on driving toward that goal.

YOUR MARKET IS INTERNATIONAL

From my desk in Amsterdam, I have observed a significant increase in international, private equity firms seeking investment opportunities in the Netherlands in recent years. A few years back, were mandated to find investors for a shared office business based in the Netherlands and were surprised at the degree of interest from abroad. In the end, a foreign investor won the deal.

Companies worldwide increasingly seek external growth in the global economy. More and more, businesses turn to cross-border transactions as a strategy for value creation. Investors are seeking higher growth markets, greater value-add products and services, and attractive valuation opportunities across borders. All of these developments increase international demand for acquisitions.

The Asian trend of rising outbound investment activity is likely to continue into the foreseeable future (though it is likely to continually evolve). Europe continues to attract inbound investment activity, as there is compelling data supporting growth's return to the Continent—growth that may not yet be fully reflected in market prices.

As I write this book, we are selling an industrial software company in North America. We have found interest among international buyers from Australia, Germany, the United Kingdom, and the United Arab Emirates. This is not unusual. Similarly, a European luxury goods manufacturer with whom we are engaged is certain to appeal to a wide range of both international strategic and financial investors.

Not long ago we sold a relatively modest-sized US gold mine with unproven gold reserves to an investor from Australia, a Danish holiday home resort to a Canadian investor, and a North American cell/mobile phone chain to a Japanese investor. The list goes on and on. The world truly is borderless when it comes to investment, and improving communications and financial technologies facilitate that investment to create a vibrant, global M&A marketplace.

Here's the point: these sales didn't happen by themselves. They were the product of an organized, disciplined, concerted international marketing effort. If a potential advisor ever pitches you that he knows the players in your arena, bear in mind the simple volume of outreach a good international marketing campaign entails. If you own a four-star hotel, for example, there are 500+ potential investors worldwide. Does he really know 500 potential buyers?

Some advisors will discount casting a wide net. They'll argue for a more targeted approach to a few strong prospects or, conversely, blasting untargeted marketing at a very large list. There can be merit in the former approach— sometimes an owner wants to minimize the potential for customers, suppliers, and competitors to know that a company is on the market, and may have some strong prospects in mind at the beginning of the research process. Even so, it's imperative that the deal team still proceeds methodically as I describe below, identifying key contacts, building a business case, and so on. We've found that regardless of how wide a net an owner wishes to cast, a methodical, research-based approach is consistently effective.

The following pyramid diagram is data from a deal involving a Manhattan-based hotel that we were mandated to sell a few years back. In the end, the owner decided not to sell due to legal and tax reasons that emerged during our marketing process. Nevertheless, this is an example of the process. We marketed to North America, Middle East, Europe, and Asia. In the end, we generated 16 expressions of interest.

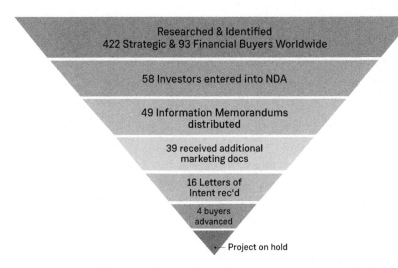

Researched & Identified
422 Strategic & 93 Financial Buyers Worldwide

58 Investors entered into NDA

49 Information Memorandums
distributed

39 received additional
marketing docs

16 Letters of
Intent rec'd

4 buyers
advanced

Project on hold

COMPONENTS OF A WELL-RUN CAMPAIGN

1. Start with research. As a business gets larger, the market of potential buyers grows—up to a point. For a typical business deal of $250 million or less (those normally handled by an M&A advisor), we'll build up a plan of who to go to and what countries to target, and we normally end up with a fairly large list. We expect to compile a list comprised of strategic and financial buyers, with strategics typically representing 85% of the list and financial buyers making up the other 15%. Depending on the nature of our client's business, we anticipate identifying anywhere from 100 to 400 potential buyers. Many of these potential buyers are not necessarily actively looking to make a purchase—but many will respond favorably to a good opportunity presented to them the right way.

To compile this list our internal research team gathers strategic names from business intelligence databases, industry and trade journals, web searches, and by asking our clients.

Details matter here. It's not enough to have the name of the company. You need the names of the various individuals within the firm, their phone numbers, their e-mail addresses, their postal addresses, even their assistants' names. Effective marketing must be effectively targeted. Otherwise, it's a waste of time.

The investor outreach team must be diligent, aggressive (in the positive sense of the word), professional, and committed to engaging with each target company. It can often be difficult to secure a telephone conversation and/or elicit an e-mail response from the individuals being targeted, so professional persistence is key. At my firm, we make eight to 10 personalized attempts for each contact at each target company before we consider them as non-responsive (for us that usually means six phone call attempts/messages and four e-mails).

Even then, we don't disqualify them. Instead, we expand our efforts to include reaching out to them via LinkedIn and send a personal e-mail from myself, the managing director. These efforts result in a relatively high response rate.

The outreach team should be led by an individual who is well spoken, personable, diligent, highly educated, mature, and committed. His or her team (usually one to three individuals) should have similar qualities. They should document all of their calls and e-mail notes in a database and provide the client with a weekly or fortnightly summary for review and discussion.

2. Fully prepare marketing materials and financials of the company before the marketing "launch." Besides creating the Information orandum and a financial analysis, we occasionally engage a professional videographer to produce a short video about the firm. Video is an incredibly powerful tool that can make the offering more memorable and compelling. Through video, prospective buyers can hear and see the seller,

CHECKLIST FOR A WELL-RUN MARKETING CAMPAIGN

- ☐ Extensive research of global strategic and financial investors
- ☐ Identify two or three target individuals for each
- ☐ Concise, compelling teaser of one to two pages
- ☐ Binding NDA signed before sending the IM
- ☐ Professionally designed IM that makes the investor want to know more
- ☐ Robust database to track call attempts for each investor
- ☐ Ask qualifying questions of prospective investors
- ☐ Create rapport and dialogue with investors
- ☐ Plant the idea of submitting an offer early
- ☐ Supplemental documents ready to go
- ☐ Professional, personable communications that build trust and respect
- ☐ Understand and position the company for synergies between seller and buyer
- ☐ Work toward a competitive bidding scenario
- ☐ Keep researching and adding prospects throughout the process
- ☐ Use data and intelligence gathered from the process to continually improve the campaign

virtually tour the facility, and begin to imagine owning the company. Whether you make a video or not, all your materials should be completely ready to go, as some investors will ask for the information immediately— often within an hour or two of the marketing launch.

3. Control the process. A competitive process requires a preplanned structure. You can't let the buyers dictate the next steps. This takes some discipline because experienced and qualified buyers will have their own ideas about what to do next. It's easy to get excited and potentially lose control.

Here's a typical scenario: a buyer seeks to pre-empt the process by trying to set up a meeting with the owners right away, or even negotiate a final price immediately. In fact, while writing this I took a call from a buyer who wanted to know the bottom-line price that a current client and I had agreed upon for my client's company. The caller just came out and asked (I have to give him credit for being direct). I was polite and said yes, we often have a ballpark bottom line selling price that we agree to with a client, but that ours is similar to an attorney-client relationship. In other words, that number isn't something I can share, nor would I, as it is not our objective to obtain the minimum selling price for our client. If he was interested, he would have to participate in the process; there would be no shortcuts here that would lead him to securing a low-bid offer. I told him if and when he puts in his first-round bid I could give him a sense of where he stood, and I was supportive and encouraging as I said it. He grumbled but agreed to follow my lead.

What I didn't tell him is that I have seen scenarios in which an excellent buyer can pre-empt the process with an extraordinary offer. I am convinced that the best price comes through competition, but I'm willing to be wrong about that if circumstances warrant. For example, on occasion a buyer may meet every one of the seller's requirements and offer a fair price. There may well be a higher bidder who offered a higher price but didn't tick off all the seller's boxes. In a case like that, if the deal on the table makes everyone happy, why not?

4. Timing is critical. You want all of your prospects to be able to reach the finish line at the same time, but not all of them move at the same speed. To manage this effectively, time your outreach. We have a tested process that we know works in terms of the timing of the different marketing channels we use. But in truth it is just common sense and careful thought.

For example, if you e-mail your strongest buyer prospects right away, they likely will respond right away. In addition, they will not need as much time to digest the opportunity as others may require because they probably already know the industry and may be familiar with the company. However, if you want to get other buyers involved you'll need to delay the process with those strongest buyers you contacted while others come up to speed. And it is rarely a good idea to stall a buyer.

Instead, a good advisor will reach out to the expected slower buyers first, then bring in the faster ones.

5. Maintain momentum. While good timing often means slowing things down just a little so all buyers can reach the finish line (bids) at the same time, good momentum means keeping things moving and taking advantage of the enthusiasm of the buyers.

Sometimes, unfortunately, some buyers get left behind. A few large corporations can barely have their legal department turn around a confidentiality agreement in the time it takes for us to go through the entire bidding process. Two months ago, we received an offer for one of our client's businesses that arrived five months after our initial engagement with them. I advised that we were in the closing stages with another buyer but if that did not conclude for any reason, we would be back in touch. The investor confessed that his firm is notoriously slow on such matters and that they often miss the boat as a result. This is frustrating, but I try to be pleasant and I'll rarely shut such a buyer down completely. Often I'll try to get them back up to speed later in the process. But some just drop out. I'd much rather keep the process going and take advantage of the momentum than stop and wait for one buyer. Losing momentum can mean losing other potential buyers.

6. Consider publishing dates. On occasion, we list the relevant milestone dates of our selling process to ensure investors are informed as to the timings. The first date after the marketing launch is when questions are due. The second is for the publication of the Q&A document and a financial update, and the third date is when that first-round bids are due. The Q&A process, in which we publish all questions and answers to all buyers, is quite powerful—it helps create a true market with better informed buyers, and it has the secondary benefit of making sure that all buyers know that there is competition (a buyer may submit five questions, yet see that we publish 100 questions and answers—they can figure out what's happening).

That said, publishing dates can be dangerous for a couple of reasons. First, there is the risk that no qualified, credible parties bid in time. In that case, your bargaining power can be greatly diminished and your credibility damaged in the eyes of potential buyers. Second and more often, there are a handful of parties that you and your advisor would view as the best buyer (the party that is likely to pay the highest price for your business) and they simply cannot move fast enough to meet the deadlines. Either of those two results runs counter to the purpose of running a sell-side M&A process.

Due to the reasons above, we often will not publish a deadline unless: (a) the deal needs to happen in a compressed timeframe (usually for per- sonal or legal reasons) or (b) the company operates in a generally transpar- ent and easily comparable market (such as hotels in global cities).

7. Keep a focus on business performance. A common factor that can wear away buyer confidence and even kill a deal is a lack of business performance during the negotiation phase. Your process should be structured so that you can continue to focus on running the business. Here's an example: typically, the sheer number of prospective buyers requiring management conference calls with the owner and management could become a resource drain and result in stalling the company. Most buyers initially want to know why you are selling, how long you plan to remain during the transition, and so on. Why subject you, the seller, to the monotony of answering these queries again and again? The solution is for the advisor to address as many of the early- and middle-stage conversations as possible, ensuring that calls and/or meetings arranged with the seller are more advanced-stage discussions. In the end, every interested buyer is going to want to meet you, your fellow shareholders, management, etc., before concluding a deal. In addition to the economics behind the business, there is the matter of ensuring the right chemistry, or "fit," between the buyer and your team.

Of course, it is inevitable that owners will experience a degree of distraction resulting from the selling process. The efforts of you and your team will be required to assist your advisor, accountant, and lawyer in the various matters to be addressed in preparing your business for sale and carrying out the process of finding the best owner for your firm. However, a good M&A advisor will minimize this workload for you, helping you to stay focused enough to essentially hit your forecasted numbers that were communicated to the buyers in the Information Memorandum and in previous discussions up to that point. The deal depends on it.

8. Let the market dictate price. Remember back in Chapter 2 when we discussed that your business is worth exactly what someone is prepared to pay for it at any given point in time? This is where the efforts of the sales and marketing come to bear in terms of how the market is valuing your business. We've had sellers that would have asked for much less than they got, sometimes tens of millions of dollars less. The flip side is that we also have concluded transactions for less than what the owners had hoped to get. However, after an exhaustive international effort to market the company to a broad market, we have the benefit of having obtained primary data from multiple buyers globally as to how they are ascribing a value to your business at that time.

EXPECTED RETURN ON INVESTMENT

Different types of investors seek vastly different return on investment. A venture capitalist may target more than 50% per year on a single investment. A private equity group may be satisfied with 25% to 35%, while a large corporation may consider 15% an acceptable return.

Why such a range? In a phrase: the cost of money.

When we first speak about how to price a business, we tend to consider multiples of earnings. But what matters to a buyer is what portion of future earnings is available to pay back the investment. Large companies, for example, typically have a fairly low cost of capital. They can raise money by selling stock or they can raise money by issuing debt. An average of these sources is called the weighted average cost of capital, or WACC. When a company looks at a purchase, they often compare the rate of return to their internal cost of raising money—their WACC. If a project returns more than the WACC, it is considered a good investment, since the company can make more money with the project than it costs to get the money. A typical WACC for a large, mature company in a low-risk area can be 8% or 10%. If they project a return on investment of 15% annually, it can look like a good deal.

On the other hand, a venture capitalist may want a 50% return because he knows he is going to flat-out lose money on most investments. He operates in a riskier world of early-stage companies and is looking for high returns from a few investments to cover his expected losses from other investments.

A high-risk technology venture with huge future potential cash flows will be discounted heavily because of the risk premium associated with that industry. Some tech ventures have enormous payoffs, but most don't. The high flyers cover the losers so the portfolio still makes a positive return. By requiring a 50% internal rate of return, the venture capitalists pad their portfolios against anticipated losses.

Private equity groups employ multilayer business models. They generally raise money from wealthy individual investors or institutional investors (or larger firms or sometimes even their family), and typically try to produce an IRR of 15% to 20% for these investors. To accomplish that they seek opportunities that produce 25% to 35% on their investment—the spread is where they make money.

9. Control the meetings. This is part of keeping owners focused on business performance, and an aspect of the M&A advisor's stagecraft. A common mistake advisors make is to accept invitations to buyer meetings as they come up, early in the process. The business owner will end up spending significant time and energy with buyers that end up offering low bid prices.

This is frustrating and disruptive. Instead, we often impose the requirement of a "first-round bid" process where each interested buyer must submit a non-binding Indication of Interest (IoI) that includes price (or at least a price range) and an indication of deal structure. We then present an analysis of the first-round bids to the client and work together to decide whom to meet with. Thus, our client knows that he or she is taking meetings only with qualified buyers who are interested in paying enough to be worth the client's time. When we do schedule meetings, we group them into a relatively tight timeframe—optimally on sequential days—to minimize disruptions to operations.

10. A signed Letter of Intent is not time to celebrate. Following the IoI, interested parties will submit their Letter of Intent (LOI). The LOI is a more formal document that contains greater detail as to the buyer's attraction toward the seller's business, an explanation why they believe they would be an appropriate new owner of the business, the investment committee's support of this acquisition and the final price to be paid. With the exception of a few provisions set out within the LOI (such as confidentiality, terms of proposed exclusivity to be granted to buyer, etc), the LOI is otherwise a non-binding offer. Typically, the LOI requires back-and-forth negotiations to arrive at an overall deal structure and price that both parties agree to. Thereafter, the document is signed by seller and buyer alike and the buyer is granted access to the data room to carry out his due diligence on the business.

It is important to note that once the parties reach an executed Letter of Intent, there is still a great deal of work ahead of everyone before you can look to reach for the Champagne. If you're a sports fan, the mutually signed LOI doesn't represent victory—it represents halftime. Once it's signed by seller and buyer, the due diligence begins, and there are plenty of ways a deal can go sideways during this process.

If your company is an attractive opportunity, is well-prepared and if your M&A advisor has done his or her job, you may likely receive multiple offers (LOIs), and you can be assured that no two offers will be the same. They will vary in their price and terms, the structure in which they are written, and their length and tone.

Once you and your advisor have selected the best buyer(s), the process of due diligence commences next. The unsuccessful bidders are advised that they won't be advancing and typically provided with detailed feedback as to why their bid failed to advance. You don't want your advisor to completely dismiss the other contenders at this stage, as you want them to stay engaged in a backup position in the event that your chosen party(ies) fail to conclude a transaction. If they've been communicated with professionally and diligently to date, then your advisor can have an open discussion with them, advising that another party has been selected to advance into exclusivity. When advising unsuccessful investors of this, we'll often extend one last opportunity to enhance their bid to secure the opportunity. They know that we are serious in our preparedness to proceed with another buyer, but that we are offering them this courtesy before doing so. Most investors are appreciative of this approach, and most often, we are able to keep the door open with them should discussions with the other investor fail to produce a successful conclusion.

ACTUALLY SELLING YOUR COMPANY

You and your team have done an enormous amount of work to get to this stage. But let's look at the effort with a critical eye: up until now, the focus was on marketing with initial stages of negotiation that led to the LOI. But now, your advisor needs to engage deeply in the process of *selling*.

But wait—you have an LOI in hand. Isn't your company effectively sold?

No. As I stated earlier, many entrepreneurs naively perceive an LOI (or term sheet, or other non-binding but important "handshake" agreement) as a "deal." We frequently hear from potential clients about how they "had a deal" in principle a few years ago, but the deal did not close for one reason or another.

That's because too many business owners—and their advisors— step back at this critical juncture. In their minds, they have done the most important task: they've brought a good offer, or set of offers, to the table. What remains is the due diligence process and drafting the definitive purchase agreements, and they (wrongly) assume they can essentially let the lawyers and accountants lead the remaining process to conclusion. But this is an enormous mistake, for there is still a great deal of due diligence work, negotiating, setting/managing expectations, controlling relationships between both sides' legal teams, focusing on driving the deal forward, and so forth. At this stage, there is still a great deal of critical work to be done to actually conclude a successful sale of your business. If you're a sports fans, the signed LOI can be likened to half-time; anything can still happen in the 2nd half. Your team still needs its coach (you), the captain (your M&A advisor) and the rest of your team engaged, focused and committed to achieving the intended end-result.

Deal making is a profession. Things do not just fall into place by accident. The skilled advisor realizes that it's his or her responsibility to finesse things into place and this is the stage where he earns his money. An advisor who is incentivized properly to get the deal over the line (lawyers and accountants are rarely are rewarded with success fees—their incentive is to bill the hours) is your strongest ally to ensure that the right deal is advanced to closing in as realistic a timeframe as possible.

NEGOTIATING TIPS

Here are a few pointers I've found useful.

- Know whom you're negotiating with. In other words, can the person across the table actually make the deal, or do they need someone else's approval?

- The first offer sets the benchmark but does not decide the deal. Don't be offended if it seems low. There's often a lot of movement after that if your team knows what they're doing.

- Have something to give away. This allows your counter-party to feel like they're getting a win in the negotiation.

- Know where your leverage is. What do you have that the other side really wants? Think synergies. It could be IP, a great client list, a geographic footprint, or something else. Figure out before you sit down what matters most to the buyer.

- Someone always controls a conversation. Better that it is you/ your advisor than the buyer dictating the rules of negotiation. Your advisor's success in having previously established a meaningful and personal dialogue with the buyer really begins to bear fruit here.

- Strive for win-win. Know the buyer's priorities, and try to walk in his shoes. Do what you can to satisfy him. For example, you may have said you'll stay on for 90 days after closing, but he'll feel better if you make it 180 days. If you can do something like that without materially hurting your position, do it. That goes a long way to-ward getting to a handshake.

- Keep cool. Be firm and professional, and maintain a neutral attitude.

After an LOI is executed, two processes begin:

1. Due diligence; and
2. Drafting of the definitive purchase agreement.

Many M&A advisors at this stage answer questions raised, but don't ask enough of their own. They accept objections instead of challenging them. They don't position the future growth prospects of their client's firm confidently. They don't build personal rapport with the potential acquirer and they don't put senior staff on the calls with the potential buyer. The lawyers and accountants may know how to write the documents, but they don't necessarily understand the personalities and friction points among the parties. In short, this is a critical stage of the process and you need to ensure that your advisor is fully engaged throughout and is confident, creative, flexible, understanding of the other side's motives, and able to navigate discussions on sticky deal points to mutual satisfaction.

Many business owners incorrectly think that due diligence is a "check the box" exercise and only a company that is dishonest would have issues. Wrong— there are always issues. Sometimes these issues are raised by the buyer in an effort to lower the valuation (or otherwise improve the deal for the buyer); sometimes they are raised because the buyer's accounting firm or the buyer may not fully understand the business (and therefore legitimately believe that a minor issue may be significant). An advisor needs to have the technical competency to analyze the impact of a misstatement, or unidentified risk area, and demonstrate when appropriate that the issue does not materially impact the deal.

The advisor also needs to confidently and intelligently manage the scope of due diligence. The buyer will almost always want a very broad scope for due diligence, without consideration of the cost to your business to support it (creation and collation of huge amounts of documents, discussions between you/your senior team and an associate from PwC about existential risks to the business, etc.).

The advisor's commitment to actively managing all of this—to selling the business—materially affects the drafting of the definitive purchase agreement. Only when that agreement is signed, and the deal is closed (i.e the money is in your bank), is your business sold. Between the signing of an LOI and closing day, there is a lot of ground to cover and multiple opportunities for the transaction to fail to conclude.

CHAPTER 8

EXCLUSIVITY AND DEAL STRUCTURE

"Expect the best, prepare for the worst."

—Zig Ziglar

Receipt of a Letter of Intent can be very exciting. For some owners it is the big, stomach-churning loop on the emotional roller coaster, an external validation of all their hard work. If the offer comes in higher than expected, that can be great news. If it comes in low, some sellers take it personally. That's a mistake. It can be hard to separate yourself from your business—but you still should do it.

When you receive a Letter of Intent, or several, don't overreact. As the LOIs come in, you will begin to gain a sense of how the world is valuing your business. As I mentioned previously, offers can—and likely will—vary considerably from one to the next. Pause for a moment and remember what you've learned as you've worked through your exit plan. It's easy to be swept up with the idea that a bird in hand is worth two in the bush, but remind yourself of why you are selling and what you want. Look hard at the deal. Go back and review your exit plan, where you wrote down the things you want. What matters to you—the highest price, a partner you can work with, the security of your employees, or something else? How does the offer you have in hand measure up against the things you have told yourself are important?

Pricing variations by 200% or more are not uncommon. This may surprise you, but as you now know, different investors will attribute different values to different aspects of your business. This is why it is so important for your advisor to position the synergies effectively with buyers and work with them to acknowledge and assign value to these synergies. The low offers can be gut-wrenching to receive, but fear not. Another offer is likely around the corner and may be double the amount of your last offer.

As I was writing this book, we closed a deal to sell a technology company. The difference between the lowest bid and the highest was 243%. As it happened, the highest bidder was not the winning party in the end. Instead, the winning investor acquired our client's business for an amount 12% less than the highest bid, owing largely to the synergies between the successful acquirer and our client's ownership and management team. It simply made more sense for them to proceed with this party, as the owner retained a minority equity stake in his business and saw enormous growth opportunities for his firm under the new majority owner's stewardship.

As this example illustrates, you almost certainly will have to make tradeoffs. So what matters most, and does this offer secure you that? What are you willing to compromise on? Consider the overall attractiveness of the deal and the risk that it may fall through (called execution risk). You may find yourself with more than one LOI, and they won't be the same. For instance, you might face the choice between a lower all-cash offer and a higher price that includes earn-out clauses, meaning you receive a percentage of the overall consideration over a period of (often) one to two years.

One client of ours received their first offer from a large, attractive buyer. Some advisors might have stopped there—they may not have been properly incentivized to get the *best* offer. Yet that first offer ended up being only 40% of the value of the deal we ended up doing with a subsequent bidder. Forty percent. Another client received 14 bids for their firm, varying 2.3X in valuation for the same asset. A third client really liked the first bid he got—but liked the 20% increase we obtained for him during negotiations even better.

My point is this: the first offer you see is often not a very good indicator of the final price. Price is only the beginning. A Letter of Intent is much more than a piece of paper stating a price the buyer is willing to pay. Such a letter generally runs to several pages and lays out multiple aspects of the deal, which I'll discuss in a moment.

With an LOI in hand, you face a critical decision: are you prepared to abandon discussions with all other interested buyers so that you can pursue a deal with the preferred (chosen) buyer? When you accept an LOI from a single buyer, that party will most often require a period of exclusivity in which you agree (and are bound by) to suspend all other marketing efforts and discussions with other interested parties for a fixed period of time (usually 45 to 90 days). Doing that has real costs, which I'll describe below. In such cases, you can only go to the dance with one date, so choose wisely.

EXPRESSION OF INTEREST VS. LETTER OF INTENT

We mentioned both before, but they warrant further consideration, as the Expressions of Interest and Letters of Intent are two similar, but slightly different, documents which cause many sellers confusion about their meaning, how binding they are, and how and when they are used.

EXPRESSION OF INTEREST (EOI)

An EOI (also referred to as an indication of interest, or IOI) is just that: an informal offer expressed in writing by a potential acquirer for the purchase of your business. Its principal purpose is to outline to the seller a range of valuation that the buyer is willing to pay. It's also an indication to the seller's advisor that the buyer has serious intent to pursue the opportunity through to a formal offer letter. Investment bankers and M&A advisors will often request an EOI in their bidding process to sort the pool of prospective buyers into a reduced, more genuine list of qualified, suitable buyers.

Along with an indicated valuation range, the EOI is likely to contain all or some of the following:

- The deal structure
- Proposed timings
- The buyer's decision-making process

EOI's are non-binding and not always part of the sales process. Some deals involve them, some don't. Much depends on the overall size of the transaction, the internal processes that the buyer may have in dealing with acquisitions, and the strategy that your advisor has adopted for the transaction process.

LETTER OF INTENT

A Letter of Intent is an official document delivered by the purchaser once they have completed their initial period of due diligence. It typically summarizes the principal points of the proposed transaction in more detail than an Expression of Interest. Although the format of LOIs varies from buyer to buyer, a typical LOI is likely to address some or all of the following:

- The purchase price, as well as any purchase price adjustments and whether any portion of the purchase price will be held in escrow
- The nature of the consideration to be paid by the buyer (cash, shares in the buyer's company, a combination of both, etc.) and any earn-out components
- The proposed transaction structure (share purchase, asset purchase, merger), including, to the degree appropriate, the exact assets that will be purchased and which are not to be purchased, any liabilities of the seller to be assumed by the buyer, and so on

- Any non-solicitation provisions ("no shop" or exclusivity provisions that we just covered above) that prohibit the seller from negotiating with other potential buyers
- The due diligence process to be undertaken by the parties, including what access the buyer will have to the seller's employees, records, and facilities
- Any conditions that must be satisfied prior to closing the transaction (for example, obtaining financing or third-party approvals, or board/shareholder approvals)
- Any non-compete provisions that may prohibit the seller from competing with the buyer in a defined geographic area for a specified period of time
- The payment of certain expenses relating to the transaction
- When the letter or term sheet will terminate

A Letter of Intent almost always non-binding. As previously mentioned, exceptions do exist and include the non-disclosure clause, and the exclusivity provision, which allows the buyer time to conduct due diligence. A buyer can (technically) be sued for providing an LOI in bad faith, but such instances are very difficult to prove.

Either party can back out of an LOI for any reason. It is uncommon for that to happen because both buyer and seller have spent significant time and money in the courtship phase leading up to the LOI. But it happens, and can go both ways. The last time it happened to me it was my client, the seller (actually the seller's brother, who was also a shareholder) who decided at the last minute not to sell. It was a personal decision relating to a family matter, but frustrating nonetheless. I had to make the difficult call to the buyer, who at that point had spent a significant amount on due diligence and was looking forward to closing the deal.

It is important for an LOI to have enough detail so there isn't a lot of negotiating left to do on major deal terms. There is always going to be some negotiating, but you really don't want to have to deal with something so major that it impacts the overall value of a deal. The LOI is a guide, or template, for the attorneys when they draft the definitive purchase agreement and other closing documents.

The LOI defines what a deal may look like, and then allows both parties time to perform due diligence. Although the buyer is spending the most time looking under the hood, the seller may conduct due diligence on the buyer if the arrangement on the table involves some sort of merger or partnership, or if the deal relies on a significant amount of financing.

Here are examples of items that I've seen missing that should be included in the LOI:

- If there is a seller note (i.e., you, the seller, agree to finance a portion of the purchase price over a specific period of time, say three years, to the purchaser of your business), the LOI should contain the terms of the note and what, if any, security is on the note. If it isn't a straight note, then a payment schedule can be helpful. For example, is that balloon payment in 2024 due at the beginning or end of 2024?
- Legal structure (asset or a stock sale).
- If there is an earn-out (future performance-based compensation), then there should be detail on how that is actually earned. If there is any confusion at all, examples can be included to show how any formulas would actually work.
- Unless the seller is going away from the business immediately after the transaction, which is rare, there should be some reference to the details on future compensation for the seller
- The status of the accounts receivable, payables, cash, etc., and any net working capital requirement should be very clear.
- How the buyer will approach the employment structure (will major changes be expected, etc.).

- Often we do deals that include continued ownership for the seller. The structure to make that happen can be complex, and, in that case, it should be clear what the new ownership is. A new ownership table ("cap table") can be helpful to include.

- Whether or not the buyer anticipates incorporating a management incentive plan for senior management team, and at least the anticipated overall structure of such.

Each LOI is different and based on the concerns of both buyer and seller. For instance, if a seller is concerned that the buyer will modify the compensation structure of the company's top salesperson during the seller's earn-out period (and thus negatively affect the earn-out), we may ask for an employment agreement to this employee that sets the compensation. You can do this after an LOI and before close, but it is usually easier to get in the LOI.

During the due diligence period, attorneys will take boilerplate purchase agreements, and similar documents and modify them according to the terms in the LOI and any other pertinent deal points to be agreed upon between the parties. A four- or five-page LOI can't possibly include all the details of an acquisition or investment, so there will be various issues to resolve. Usually, most of these points can be resolved quickly and amicably, but many items may be more challenging to figure out, and thus, give rise to prolonged discussions and negotiations between the parties. At this stage, the buyer and seller are motivated to complete a deal and momentum is in both parties' favor. However, that doesn't mean that genuine difference in interpretations and/or opinions cannot and will not arise, and that you may find yourself engaged in debates on points that you had not previously considered would be a sticking point.

CLOSING BALANCE SHEET ADJUSTMENTS

One such area is that of working capital. Working capital is an issue with most M&A transactions. A common mistake is to avoid addressing this during the LOI phase. Purchase price adjustments related to working capital (i.e., paying more or less based on the specific balance sheet of the seller on closing) can easily swing the purchase price by significant amounts and therefore this should be considered in the assessment of an offer made pre-LOI (for comparison purposes, for example).

It's typical to see an inclusion in the definitive purchase agreement that relates to closing balance sheet adjustments. Day-to-day changes in working capital are unavoidable, so purchase agreements must account for them. Be aware of tactics that may be employed by a buyer to exploit closing balance sheet adjustments as a means to recapture a portion of the agreed-upon purchase price.

Most transactions are structured on a "cash-free, debt-free" basis. Often a buyer's strategy will include leverage, and those buyers require debt-free companies so that they use the assets as collateral for debt financing. This means that the buyer does not pay you for cash or marketable securities, and does not assume any long-term debt as part of the transaction. On the day of closing, any excess cash and cash equivalents on the balance sheet will increase the purchase price dollar-for-dollar, while the seller will be responsible for paying off all long-term debt. Receivables, payables, and working capital related items typically remain with the company (i.e., the buyer) as necessary components of the ongoing balance sheet.

The key to these calculations not becoming an issue on the day of closing is to address them in the LOI or pre-LOI. Purchase price adjustments (i.e., paying more or less based on the specific balance sheet of the seller on closing) can easily swing the purchase price multiple millions of dollars.

There are two basic elements for determining how to handle working capital and purchase price adjustments:

- **Working capital peg:** Set a required amount of working capital required for the business to be sufficiently capitalized, and any amount in excess or deficit impacts the purchase price on closing.
- **Cash free, debt free:** the buyer does not assume any of the debt on the seller's balance sheet, nor will the buyer get to keep any cash on the seller's balance sheet.

Both of the above are conceptually reasonable. However, the business owner and advisor need to discuss and understand the impact of the methods and whether the seller is likely to be penalized or benefited by one or the other. Examples of differences would include where there is a volatile mix between cash and accounts receivable (often happens when there are a relatively small number of transactions with high dollar amounts), the capital intensity of the seller, historic and closing short-term debt, etc.

Seasonality of the business also needs to be considered. Companies may require more working capital during specific times of the year, and that should be factored into the analysis and negotiation of an LOI and definitive agreement.

DEAL STRUCTURE: TWO BASIC TYPES

If you're selling your business (rather than merging, for example), you are transferring assets in some form, because ultimately that's what a business is—a collection of assets. The purchase agreements to acquire those assets take two general forms: Share Purchase Agreement (SPA) and Asset Purchase Agreement (APA).

SHARE PURCHASE AGREEMENT

In a Share Purchase transaction, the seller removes himself or herself from the company, allowing the buyer to step directly into the shoes of the seller. The business proceeds without interruption. Normally, the seller will prefer a Share (stock) Purchase over an Asset Purchase transaction. This is because under a Share Purchase Agreement, the whole company (including any liability) transfers to the buyer and the seller typically receives more advantageous tax treatment over the transaction. The buyer, however, will usually seek an Asset Purchase because it enables the buyer to pick only the assets he wants to acquire (while avoiding any undesirable liabilities), while simultaneously exploiting more favorable tax treatment.

One of the principal arguments for a Share Purchase Agreement is that the buyer will continue the operation of the company, in the same corporate form, as the seller. In other words, there is no new entity operating the business of the company. The company name lives on and its place of business remains unchanged. Employees remain in place with the company and everything stays the same except the owner's identity. The continuation of the company typically means that third-party consent for the transfer of contracts is not required. (Note that consent can be required if a contract has a "change of control" clause.) For these reasons, a Share Purchase transaction can facilitate a seamless transition for clients and/or employees. For many sellers, this is the preferred route as it ensures the least disruption to staff and customers.

Under the terms of a typical SPA, the seller will indemnify the buyer against any pre-transaction liabilities of the company. This is a standard and entirely reasonable request from buyers. After all, who wants a nasty surprise after closing? If, for example, a government agency determines that the company owes back taxes from the time when the seller controlled the business, the seller should be responsible for paying those taxes. The same holds true for any customer or employee disputes or other potential liabilities that originated prior to date of closing. SPAs incorporate standard indemnification language that protects the buyer from such occurrences.

Unless the parties have specifically agreed to the contrary in the Share Purchase Agreement, following the sale of the company, the seller will have no continuing interest in the company, the assets, or the ongoing business. The exception to this may be when the parties agree to the seller's continued involvement post-transaction—for instance, when an earn-out is involved. As I'll discuss in the next chapter, earn-out structures can be designed in various ways, and may mean that the seller retains a vested interest in the company during the term of the earn-out.

A Share Purchase has certain advantages:

- A Share Purchase can be more straightforward and quicker than an Asset Purchase
- No transfers of title to assets are required
- No need to transfer contracts to the buyer, so typically no third-party consent is required and less disruption in the business occurs
- Tax-loss carryforwards may be preserved and utilized by the buyer
- Buyer gets the "goodwill" and past performance record of the seller

And disadvantages (for the buyer):

- Liabilities of the seller will automatically carry over to the buyer.
- Buyer cannot "cherry pick" the assets it wants to acquire and avoid the assets it does not want.
- Buyer takes the seller's tax basis in the purchased assets—not a "stepped-up" basis.

ASSET PURCHASE AGREEMENT

In an Asset Purchase, the buyer purchases some or all of the assets of the target company. The main benefit of an Asset Purchase is that the buyer has the flexibility to pick and choose the assets and liabilities it wishes to acquire, leaving behind those it does not want. This structure is often used, for example, when acquiring a single business unit within a company, such as a division. The seller retains ownership of the shares of the entity, and the buyer typically forms a new entity for the assets they have acquired.

An asset purchase may also allow the buyer to exclude certain liabilities the buyer does not want to assume. However, some liabilities (including some environmental liabilities) may transfer with the business by law, even if excluded by contract. Structuring a transaction as an asset purchase generally involves more legal work than a share purchase or merger.

Some assets, such as machinery and inventory, may be easy to transfer via a simple bill of sale. Certain other assets, however, require considerably more effort. Identifying all required third-party consents at an early stage will help avoid delays at closing. Certain licenses and permits may require government approval before you may transfer them to the buyer. Intellectual property, such as trademarks and patents, often requires a separate assignment and recordation with the appropriate government office. Transfers of real estate usually require title insurance and recording a deed. Or you may need to obtain third-party consent in order to properly transfer certain assets to the buyer. For instance, if the buyer wishes to acquire a contract that contains a "no assignment" provision, the contract counterparty must consent before the transfer can be completed. Contract counterparties may even view this as an opportunity to renegotiate the terms of the contract or extract concessions. Your team may expend considerable time and effort to obtain these consents.

An asset purchase has certain advantages:

- Because buyers prefer asset purchases, the terms often will result in a higher purchase price than a share purchase.
- The buyer can avoid the purchase of unwanted assets.
- In a purchase of assets, the buyer can avoid inheriting any disadvantageous tax position the seller's corporation may have.
- The buyer can take advantage of a "stepped-up basis" for valuing balance sheet assets and deduct them for tax purposes over a number of years.
- The buyer can avoid inadvertently assuming or taking title subject to certain liabilities.

And disadvantages:

- If the seller is a corporation, gain on the sale of assets will be taxed to the corporation and any distributions of the proceeds to the shareholders will be taxed to the shareholders (a stock would prevent this double taxation).
- Depending on the jurisdiction, some of the sale may be taxed as ordinary income rather than capital gains.
- The seller has the problem of disposing of unsold assets.
- The seller has to unwind the company and may still be exposed to certain liabilities.

WHAT ABOUT MERGERS?

In a merger, the buyer and the seller join forces through a merger agreement into a single legal entity. The shareholders of the target (seller's) company will receive the shares of the buyer company, cash, or a combination of stock and cash. This is often done using a new subsidiary created by the buyer to be merged with the target. This is called a "triangular merger" because there are three parties: the buyer, the buyer's subsidiary, and the target.

A merger is similar to a share purchase in that assets transfer automatically without the need for third-party consents (except in the case of "change of control" provisions as mentioned above). Also, the buyer acquires all liabilities, known and unknown, of the target company. One advantage of a merger transaction is that it can usually be accomplished with the consent of the holders of a majority of the target company's shares. This is in contrast to a share purchase, in which every shareholder must consent to a sale of its stock. Dissenting shareholders, however, may have "appraisal rights" allowing them to request that a court determine the fair value for their shares.

A merger is a more complex process if the target company is a public company. The buyer will require the shareholders' consent to the merger. To obtain this consent, a shareholders' meeting must be held so that the shareholders can vote for the merger, and the buyer and seller will have to coordinate the preparation for that meeting and the solicitation of share-holder proxies to vote in favor of the merger.

SPA VS. APA: WHICH IS RIGHT FOR YOU?

Assuming you're not merging with your buyer (and in most cases, even if the firms are combining the deal, structure will likely be an Asset or Share Purchase), you face a choice between a Share Purchase and an Asset Purchase. It's not necessarily an easy or straightforward decision. As the seller, you and your advisor have some bargaining power to dictate how you wish the sale to proceed, but this will require some forethought re-garding the legal, tax, and personal consequences of each approach. This strategic mapping should involve your legal and tax team. Early collabo-ration is the best way to make sure you're protecting your interests with the right structure for you. The truth is, though, you should aim to create a structure that is not only beneficial to you, but also to your potential buyer. Transaction structure may be complicated, and the benefits of a structure for one party may work to the disadvantage of the other party. To get a good deal done, both parties and their attorneys must weigh the competing legal, tax, and business considerations and creatively construct the most mutually advantageous transaction structure.

ESCROW/INDEMNIFICATION

Escrow and indemnification considerations often are put on hold until lawyers begin drafting the definitive purchase agreement. Buyers generally don't want to specify their commitments on such matters until they've conducted serious due diligence. However, a savvy seller in a competitive bidding environment can push for these terms to be specified in the LOI. That can increase the seller's confidence in the shape of the likely final agreement. Even though the LOI isn't binding, a serious buyer won't try to deviate from it unless something unexpected surfaces during due diligence.

If you have the leverage to ask for it, consider asking for these items in the Letter of Intent:

- **Escrow Amount:** Many transactions generally require an 8% to 15% "holdback" of the purchase price in escrow for potential claims against ordinary representations and warranties that may arise after closing.
- **Survival Period:** The period of time buyers are allowed to make claims against the seller's ordinary representations and warranties (typically 12 to 24 months).
- **Indemnification Threshold:** A minimum level of potential losses from claims made by the buyer before making a claim

against the escrow. Having a threshold of 10% to 20% of the escrow amount can help avoid minor post-closing disputes.

BUYER EXCLUSIVITY

When you sign a Letter of Intent, you often agree to grant the buyer an exclusive period to examine your company. For all intents and purposes, you cease the marketing and sales process. While this demand for exclusivity is reasonable and logical, a savvy or unscrupulous buyer can turn it to their advantage.

Consider this scenario:

I once had a conversation with the owner of an attractive piece of property that was ripe for redevelopment. He had acquired the property years earlier with his brother, and now the two were ready to sell. For various reasons stemming from the fact that they simply did not have the time to do so, they decided to forego hiring an advisor and running a formal process in which numerous potential acquirers would be engaged to determine their respective interest.

A foreign investor approached them with an attractive offering price of $45 million. The offer was conditioned by the buyer's insistence on exclusivity for 60 days while he conducted his due diligence. This meant that the owners were not allowed to hold discussions with any other investors during this period; to do so would create a breach of contract.

They were very happy with the offer and granted the buyer the 60-day exclusivity period.

After two months of answering countless requests for data, on-site meetings with the buyer, his advisors, technical team, architects, and engineers, the buyer came back singing a very different song. He explained that the due diligence exercise had yielded several areas of concern regarding the project and that the offer, in consideration of these developments, must be reduced to $28 million to compensate for the added complexity, costs, extended timelines. That's a 38% reduction in the initial price. It was significant enough to kill the deal. The brothers had wasted two months and a lot of money and energy.

I don't know the buyer personally, but I'll bet dollars to donuts that he never intended to acquire the property at $45 million. Rather, he came in with an attractive offer to a motivated seller who was not being well advised, and took advantage of the situation to secure two months of exclusivity. The buyer had little to lose and much to gain if he could wear the seller down through the due diligence process, then make convincing arguments about how that process had revealed significant concerns and those warranted a material reduction in price.

Because the sellers gave up control of the process to the buyer (although you could argue that by failing to hire an advisor they never had control of the process to begin with), they lost the ability to negotiate with other buyers that would have yielded them more attractive prospects. I've said it before and I'll say it again: the single most important element to successfully concluding a favorable transaction is to create a competitive bidding situation. If a bidder is aware that they are the only suitor, expect them to take advantage of this situation in one way or another.

THE DUE DILIGENCE PROCESS

With the Letter of Intent signed, the buyer and seller get down to due diligence. This process includes detailed analysis of your company's financial records, operations, details of key customers, marketing strategies, facilities, legal and tax records, employees, and so on. Any issues or concerns that a buyer uncovers during the due diligence period are likely to produce a reduction in price offered, less advantageous deal terms, or worse, the buyer walking away.

From a buyer's perspective, due diligence is a detective game, and they are likely to have very good detectives on their team. They won't just look under the hood; they will know specifically what they're seeking and will have the acumen to know what they're seeing. The goal of due diligence is to make the buyer comfortable enough that he goes through with the deal and closes.

Expect them to look for deal-breakers and deal-amenders alike: problems that force them to abandon to acquisition, and issues that provide a basis for changes in the structure, terms, or price of the deal. They'll examine the "hard" and "soft" aspects of your business alike. (Financials won't mean much post-transaction if they can't retain your key team members who made those financials happen.)

Sophisticated buyers will have people on their team trained to look for issues that others may miss. It's important, therefore, to ensure that your advisors have fully disclosed all material issues and threats in your company prior to signing a Letter of Intent. No buyer wants negative surprises at this stage of advanced discussions. Such developments inevitably lead to questions such as "what else am I missing?" and "why did they not disclose this to us earlier?" Those questions erode the credibility and integrity of the deal and ultimately, your own personal integrity.

Buyers often have other partners (usually banks or private equity firms) who are providing some of the financing, and have stricter requirements than the buyer does. You may be confronted with the requirement to overcome both the buyer's demands and the buyer's financial partner's demands.

Due diligence typically begins as soon as the Letter of Intent is signed. Many sellers are unprepared for this stage, failing to comprehend the sheer volume of data they have to prepare, collate, and make available to the investor. It can be a daunting exercise. You and your team will have to provide most of the information, but your M&A advisor should shoulder the majority of the organizational burden. He will provide a list of the information required from you, index it, and upload it to an electronic data room that the buyer can access via a password.

* * *

In order to keep the momentum moving in the right direction, all due diligence information should be ready and available for the buyer the moment both parties have signed the LOI.

Many sellers rightly want to know how much time they should allocate to gathering information. Of course, the process can vary widely between two companies, and your advisor's efficiency in this respect will also determine how lengthy and burdensome a process it will be. We typically allocate one month for a seller to compile the data required. Much of the information will come from different personnel within your company: CEO, CFO, HR, IT, Legal, Accounting, and so on. They have other priorities to tend to, so they'll need some lead time to gather data.

The best and most efficient approach looks something like this:

- Your advisor provides a comprehensive Excel spreadsheet of the information required for the data room, including detailed descriptions where necessary, of each piece of data requested.
- You assign each item on the list to the appropriate staff member, along with a deadline that affords you a one-week buffer (in case of delivery delays).
- As data is compiled you check it off your list and forward it directly to your advisor, who organizes it in Dropbox or a secure data room.

Remember, start this process as soon the sales and marketing phase commences. This way, by time an LOI has been signed, the data room can be fully prepared and waiting for due diligence to begin.

Here's a summary of the 20 significant areas you can expect buyers to want to explore. For more information on this topic, feel free to email us at *ExitSupport@markcarmichael.com* or visit *www.markcarmichael.com*.

1. Financial Matters: All your company's historical financial statements and related financial metrics, as well as the reasonability of your projections of future performance.

2. Technology/Intellectual Property: The extent and quality of your company's technology and IP, and evidence of any related measures taken to protect such IP (patents, copyrights, trademarks, etc.).

3. Customers/Sales: Your company's customer base, including the level of concentration of the largest customers and the sales pipeline.

4. Strategic Fit with Buyer: The buyer will want to understand the extent to which the company will fit strategically within their organization.

5. Material Contracts: One of the most time-consuming (but critical) components of a due diligence inquiry is the review of all material contracts and commitments.

6. Employee/Management Issues: The buyer will want to understand the quality of your company's management and employee base.

7. Litigation: An overview of any litigation (pending, threatened, or settled), arbitration, or regulatory proceedings involving your company.

8. Tax Matters: Tax due diligence may or may not be critical, depending on the historical operations of your company, but even for companies that have not incurred historical income tax liabilities, an understanding of any tax carryforwards and their potential benefit to the buyer may be important.

9. Antitrust and Regulatory Issues: Antitrust and regulatory scrutiny of acquisitions has been increasing in recent years.

10. Insurance: A review of key insurance policies of your company's business.

11. General Corporate Matters: Counsel for the buyer will invariably undertake a careful review of the organizational documents and general corporate records (including capitalization) of your company.

12. Environmental Issues: The buyer will want to analyze any potential environmental issues your company may face, the scope of which will depend on the nature of its business.

13. Related-Party Transactions: The buyer will be interested in understanding the extent of any "related-party" transactions, such as agreements or arrangements between your company and any current or former officer, director, stockholder, or employee.

14. Governmental Regulations, Filings, and Compliance: The buyer will want to understand the extent to which your company is subject to and has complied with regulatory requirements.

15. Property: A review of all property owned by your company or otherwise used in the business.

16. Production-Related Matters: Depending on the nature of your company's business, the buyer will often undertake a review of your company's production-related matters.

17. Marketing Arrangements: The buyer will want to understand your company's marketing strategies and arrangements.

18. Competitive Landscape: The buyer will want to understand the competitive environment in which your company's business operates.

19. Online Data Room: It is critically important to the success of a due diligence investigation that your company establish, maintain, and update as appropriate a well-organized, online data room to enable the buyer to conduct due diligence in an orderly fashion.

20. Working Capital Requirements: The buyer will want to understand the capital intensity of the business—that is, the amount of resources that your company requires to effectively cover the usual costs and expenses necessary to produce goods or provide the services that generate revenue. They want to know the risks and variances such as seasonality or major divergences in when or how the company pays its suppliers and is paid by its customers, etc. It is critical that you and your advisor understand any adjustments that should be made to GAAP/IFRS financial statements to reflect the reality of the business (in many cases, for example, deferred support revenue for software companies are not true liabilities and mutual understanding of this would be required to structure appropriate working capital adjustments on closing).

DATA ROOMS

The extent of information and level of detail in the data room should be balanced, providing enough information to enable buyers to determine a fair value but also limiting the amount of sensitive or competitive information disclosed to anyone other than the ultimate purchaser.

A comprehensive, well-thought-out data room demonstrates to buyers that your company has the tools, resources, systems, and abilities to analyze the business and track the information needed to grow and safeguard profits. Conversely, a poorly assembled data room with significant information gaps signals potential buyers that there may be operational or other data weaknesses that could dampen their views on value.

A data room used to be just that—an actual room in an attorney's office, secured by your legal team. Today, data rooms almost always take the form of online information hubs. They might be as simple as a password-protected folder on Dropbox, but there are a variety of online secure data room services that create a trail of who has accessed the information when, what documents they have viewed, and so forth. Online data rooms speed the process, lower costs, and better manage information flow by, among other things, restricting access to certain information based upon where in the process potential buyers are. You may also limit access based on the type of buyer—for instance, you can likely provide certain information to a financial buyer earlier in the process than you would with a direct competitor who is considering acquiring you.

The data room typically brings together comprehensive information covering financial results, key business drivers, legal affairs, organizational structure, contracts, information systems, insurance coverage, environmental matters, and human resources issues like employment agreements and benefit and pension plans. As I noted, your team should begin pulling together this information as soon as the Confidential Information Memorandum is drafted. The material in the data room, after all, supports the IM.

When due diligence is complete, if everything has gone well, you will get what you have worked so hard for: a final and binding offer.

In transactions such as "mergers of equals" and transactions in which the transaction includes a significant amount of the stock of the buyer, or such stock comprises a significant portion of the overall consideration, your company may want to engage in "reverse diligence." This may be as broad in scope as the primary diligence conducted by the buyer. Many or all of the activities and issues described here will, in such circumstances, apply to both sides of the transaction.

CHAPTER 9

WHAT ARE EARN-OUTS?

"The best way to predict the future is to create it."

—Peter Drucker

An earnout is a contingent portion of the purchase price which the seller and buyer agree will be paid after the closing of a transaction but which is based on the business achieving particular goals or milestones.

These milestones are normally financial in nature, such as achieving a particular revenue or EBITDA target during a defined period. They can also be based on operational milestones such as entering a new market or obtaining regulatory approval for a product.

Buyers purchase businesses for future earnings. But those earnings are not guaranteed, and in growing companies they can be hard (or impossible) to predict. An earn-out is a hedge by the buyer—a future payment to the seller, based on the business achieving defined performance milestones. Earn-outs often require the seller, as part of the purchase agreement, to remain with the company for a set period of time.

For example, in a simple earn-out arrangement, a seller may agree to continue to work at the company for 18 months after the transaction closes. If the seller grows the company by an additional $10 million in revenue (assuming that certain margins and other fundamental financial metrics are maintained), he will be paid an additional $10 million by the new owner.

Earn-out discussions naturally arise when there is a significant difference between historical earnings and future projections. Whereas a seller says, "trust me," the buyer responds, "show me." An earn-out lets the seller prove the company's value while being compensated for doing so. For many owners, the thought of remaining at the helm, under new ownership and with access to their balance sheet, customer base, more sophisticated marketing and sales channels, etc., is an enticing one. However, it all comes down to the individual entrepreneur himself/herself. If you're intent on walking away from the business and going on an extended holiday, then the thought of staying behind to steward the company yet longer is un- likely to entice you.

SRS Acquiom, an M&A transaction support platform, noted that in 2020, 19% of M&A transactions included an earnout. The median earnout potential, calculated as the amount of the potential earnout payment over the amount paid at closing was 39%. 81% of all earnouts involved an earnout period of less than 3 years post-closing, with 52% of all earnouts being 2 years or less after closing.

There are many good reasons to include an earn-out in a deal. However, an earn-out clause is not a guarantee. Every seller who agrees to one must accept the risk that they may not be paid anything at all if the business fails to achieve its agreed-upon milestones.

EARN-OUT SCENARIOS

SCENARIO 1: STABLE EARNINGS

This company has a stable history and a credible projection. In other words, the risk to the buyer is fairly low. An earn-out doesn't make sense here. The purchase terms should be cash and possibly a note, but unless there are other risks, the note shouldn't be contingent on revenue or earnings. Buyers may still push for earn-outs to mitigate their overall risk, so if you feel an earn-out is unjustified, make sure your advisor stands his ground and dismisses the notion of an earn-out early on.

SCENARIO 2: SUPPORTED GROWTH

The projected future growth is clearly supported by historical trends. But who is going to benefit from the growth? A seller may say, "You can see what will happen, so I feel that the business should be valued with a high EBITDA multiple, or possibly use next year's earnings."

The buyer may counter that growth will be a result of his post-purchase efforts, not the seller's work. A smart seller will respond that much of the expected future growth will be built upon the foundation he laid. The pipeline, recurring revenue, the company's brand, website, reputation, product, service, and other components have all come together to build momentum. However, he is also asking the buyer to trust him, which is unlikely.

Here's where an earn-out comes into play, and what it could look like: A "base price" of cash and notes calculated using historical performance, plus an earn-out structure based on the company hitting certain targets. The targets may be revenue or earnings milestones, but they can be anything the parties agree to.

SCENARIO 3: UNSUPPORTED GROWTH

An owner may believe there is a lot of growth potential, even though he hasn't taken advantage of it. For instance, he might be selling products in a brick-and-mortar store and know that he could do a lot more business if he started selling online, too.

In this case the owner doesn't stand much of a chance for an earn-out. The buyer can assert that if he does the work to capture that new growth, he should benefit. The prospect of an earn-out here is low.

SCENARIO 4: RECESSION-PROOFING A TRANSACTION

While earn-outs are most common in transactions involving growing companies, some buyers want them as insurance for more stable companies during economic downturns. Buyers don't mind if the recession has reduced sales prior to closing the transaction (that can lower the price they pay). But they won't be happy with further sales reductions after they close. In such a situation, a buyer may set a lower base number with an earn-out based on revenues (or a similar metric) remaining stable.

HOW OFTEN ARE EARN-OUTS USED?

An American Bar Association Deal Points Study (2020-21) revealed that earn-outs appeared in 20% of post-pandemic transactions, the lowest percentage in the last decade by 5-8% (these deals involved upper-middle-market companies valued at $20 million to $100 million). In Europe, the results were largely the same, with CMS' European M&A Study 2021 revealing that 21% of deals included earnouts.

Small business transactions generally don't employ earn-outs in transactions, since sellers generally don't stay on very long during transitions. The financials of these businesses can be somewhat messy, so measuring earn-out milestones is problematic. Finally, buyers usually want to come in and operate the business as theirs without any of the operating limitations that often occur with an earn-out arrangement.

Earn-outs are fairly common for larger companies in the lower-middle market and middle market. Valuation gaps between buyers and sellers are common, and that naturally leads to discussions about an earn-out.

That said, earn-outs sometimes disappear during subsequent negotiations when the challenges of actually structuring the earn-out become apparent.

Typical issues that need to be worked out include figuring how to measure the earn-out, how long to make the earn-out period, and what operational limitations will be placed on the buyer.

For example, I oncemanaged a deal that initially involved an earn-out. During last-minute negotiations, with two buyers still left bidding, one of the buyers dropped the earn-out and made that portion of the payment a non-contingent note. That swung the deal his way; the next day the seller signed that buyer's LOI.

EARN-OUT PERIOD

Earn-out periods of 12 to 24 months are the most common. The length of the earn-out often depends on how long the seller remains involved in the business. Naturally, the seller wants some control of the company during the earn-out period to make sure the company achieves the targets. The earn-out period shouldn't be too short, as that gives the buyer an incentive to defer short-term revenue in order to avoid paying an earn-out. Too long, and the earn-out can delay the impact of the purchase for the buyer.

BASIS FOR EARN-OUTS

This number varies widely, as it's a function of how much earnings risk the buyer is trying to mitigate. I've seen earn-outs ranging from 10% to 50% of the purchase price, although 10% to 25% is more common.

A buyer will commonly wish to base an earn-out on EBITDA because, after all, that is really what he cares about. But a seller fears that, even if he is still actively working in the business, he will not have complete control over costs and therefore cannot control EBITDA. (An experienced deal attorney I know in Dubai once told me this issue causes the most lawsuits after a deal is closed.) The solution is usually to negotiate earn-outs based on revenue milestones, *not* EBITDA. Gross margins can also work. In other words, the general rule is that the further up the profit and loss statement you go, the easier it is to measure earn-out.

Earn-outs can also be assessed on other major milestones such as signing (or re-signing) a major contract, getting government approval or launching a new product.

Keep in mind that the goal should be simplicity, although conversations on these matters often start with the best of intentions and then derail as both parties begin to assess the ramifications of the proposed earn-out structure. Complex formulas based on revenue, gross margins or earnings are problematic when it comes to actually writing a purchase agreement and making sure that, months later, everyone who reads it will come away with the exact same understanding. It's easy to brainstorm and draw graphs and curves, and to talk about cliffs and caps. But complex earn-out models often do not translate well into a legal agreement.

CONTROLS AND RESTRICTIONS

Early in the earn-out conversation, be sure to discuss these items:

- **Exact metric(s) for earn-out:** As the seller, the higher up the income statement you are as it relates to your earn-out, the better. Earn-outs based upon top line revenue are more difficult to dispute than other performance metrics (such as gross profit, earnings, or EBITDA). After the transaction closes, you no longer retain control of expenses.
- **Excluded items:** Earn-outs are occasionally proposed based on sales from specific customers or current product lines. By limiting the earn-out to specific business channels, an inherent

conflict of interest is created that increases the possibility of a post-closing dispute. For example, if new ownership has the opportunity to avoid paying a sizeable earn-out by selling to an excluded customer (even a less-profitable one), the decision may be influenced by the chance to avoid making that payment.

- **Collars and flexibility**: Earn-outs that are contingent upon achieving specific performance targets can also cause problems in the future. For example, suppose you have an earn-out provision in the purchase agreement that states "$1.5 million shall be paid to Seller for each fiscal year in which overall sales exceed $30 million over the next three fiscal years." Can you see the potential negative incentive for the new owner? Hint: it has to do with the last dollar of revenue required to cross the $30 million hurdle, which might lead to the new owner managing the firm's revenue if the $30 million threshold is approaching near the end of the fiscal year. If he defers the additional revenue into the following fiscal year, he saves himself a $1.5 million payment to you.

The point is this: the earn-out payment schedule must be well thought out, regardless of the metrics you agree to use.

When a buyer proposes an earn-out, a seller gets a say about the conditions. For example, if the metric is 15% growth the following year, the seller may demand:

- The office will stay in the same location
- Key employees will not be terminated
- The sales compensation structure will remain the same
- A certain amount of capital will be invested in a project

However, each restriction is a negotiation in itself, which is another reason to keep everything as simple as possible. For example, it is easy to say that a key employee cannot be terminated, but what if he commits fraud?

You can say that sales compensation will remain the same, but maybe the new company uses a different healthcare package—does this change the compensation? In other words, the issues that need to be solved in earn-outs tend to run much deeper than anticipated. As I previously noted, it's common for earn-outs to disappear late in negotiations when the parties figure out there are just too many issues to address.

CHAPTER 10

THE SALE & PURCHASE AGREEMENT AND CLOSING

KEEP CALM
AND
CLOSE THE DEAL

A few years ago, we were in the closing stage of a deal when it became obvious that the lawyers for both sides were going to debate virtually every single word of the Share Purchase Agreement. This extreme case of over-lawyering had gone on for four weeks and ran the risk of killing the deal.

We advised both our seller and the buyer CEO that the lawyers were causing unnecessary delays and expense—and more significantly, were putting the outcome of the transaction at risk. At an all-hands-on-deck meeting, the CEOs of both sides asked the lawyers to explain themselves. The resulting discomfort was quite effective. Both CEOs made it very clear, in no uncertain terms, that the time for such conduct was up and that they should proceed to immediate closing. Our client went so far as put his law firm on formal notice and demand a full accounting of the matter. He ended up with a 35% reduction in his legal bill.

Such drama isn't that common, but the risks of a deal going sideways for any number of reasons are real. You and your advisor have to stay in the game to keep everyone driving toward the goal. You now have in your sights "Day One"—the date upon which the buyer will become the legal owner of your company (or, if it's a merger, in which you join into a single entity). You, the buyer, and your advisors are driving toward creating and signing the definitive purchase agreements that are a substantial step toward making Day One a reality.

In the old days (and in movies), closings were dramatic events in which everyone gathered in a corporate boardroom with expensive fountain pens in hand. In reality, most closings happen via digital signatures/e-mail and FedEx. They are executed through the exchange of signed documents by e-mail, followed up by registered delivery of the original hard copies. This is certainly more convenient than traveling to a closing, but it does require more advance planning and can become a logistical nightmare if the process is not completely thought through, particularly when many parties, or third parties not affiliated with the buyer or seller, are involved.

A well-organised closing should be reasonably straightforward, but the importance of adequate preparation and planning cannot be overestimated. Yours and the buyer's lawyers will be driving the process forward, but don't adapt a passive role during this stage. If your advisor is experienced, they can look after your interests while maintaining healthy communications with the lawyers on both sides, ensuring that all details are being appropriately addressed. Your role is to trust, but verify.

The definitive purchase agreement that you will sign at closing formally transfers ownership of the firm. It outlines in detail the terms and conditions for the sale of your company. It addresses issues and conditions on behalf of both the seller and the buyer. These include the payment terms/ structure of the transaction, the representations and warranties, termination clause, and other essential considerations.

These agreements normally include clauses addressing:

- Assets/Shares purchased
- Trade name and property transfer
- Purchase consideration
- Terms of payment
- Obligations
- Warranties and covenants made by both parties
- Deliveries
- Liabilities
- Indemnities
- Compliances
- Closing conditions
- Termination and defaults

As the seller of your business, consider which party prepares the first draft of a definitive purchase agreement. Whichever side does this—usually the buyer—gains the opportunity to incorporate terms favorable to the drafting party. The buyer thus effectively sets the pace for negotiating the definitive agreement. A seller may question this—but bear in mind that writing the first draft can be a fairly lengthy process, requiring considerable time from a lawyer. Thus, the benefit of preparing the first draft is counterbalanced by higher legal costs typically associated with it.

CLOSING STAGE TO-DOS

When the day comes to execute (sign) the SPA, it may be associated with the simultaneous closing of the deal OR it may involve a deferred closing in which the parties have previously agreed there will be a necessary gap in time between signing and closing.

Deferred closings are not uncommon and can be required for a number of reasons, including any necessary regulatory approvals or third-party consents that may be required in the change of ownership of your business. If this is the case in your transaction, your lawyer and advisor will be able to clearly explain the basis for the deferred closing to you and the associated timings before the deal can close.

In any event, the signed purchase agreement is a major milestone in your exit process, as the contractual terms and conditions of the transaction are now completed and binding between the parties.

You don't want to rush a closing—but you don't want to let things drag either. "Deal fatigue" can be detrimental to your interests. My team has heard me say it a thousand times: Time is the killer of all deals.

Also, the passage of time allows for potential external factors beyond your control to potentially impact the eventual closing. Consider political events that may have an impact on the economy and/or the buyer's business; recall how covid-19 threw the world into chaos and uncertainty; key decision-makers in the deal can become ill, injured or die. The list goes on. Time is the killer of all deals, so both parties should maintain a healthy bias toward closing the deal as soon as is reasonably possible.

When it comes to closings, first and foremost, you need a closing checklist. This is a must-have for seller and buyer alike. Typically, the buyer's lawyer drafts and circulates this. If that doesn't happen, ask your advisor (not your attorney), to draft a list—*then* ask your attorney to review it. This saves legal fees.

We always recommend that the checklist be mutually agreed upon and distributed to the relevant parties on both sides. Almost certainly, the buyer will have their own checklist, too, but it makes sense to ensure that the seller and buyer are working off the same list and are in agreement as to where matters stand as the closing approaches. Setting and managing expectations here is paramount to ensuring an effective process.

The checklist should define each document to be signed, the status of the document until it is ready for signature, and who needs to sign it. Your M&A advisor should maintain the checklist, updating it daily and staying on top of the relevant parties who are responsible.

Your advisor should be driving the process forward on your behalf at this point. During this time there may be outstanding tax matters, financial planning issues, or other legal issues to be resolved. Expect all the deal team members on both sides to be working hard to get to Day One. When you are checking an advisor's references, ask specifically about how involved he or she remained during the closing process, and who took the lead in bringing the closing to fruition.

REPRESENTATIONS AND WARRANTIES

In both a Share Purchase Agreement and Asset Purchase Agreement, the seller and buyer alike must make certain representations and warranties as of the closing date and agree to certain covenants that will bind them before and after closing.

The "reps and warranties" sections tend to be among the most negotiated parts of the agreement, which makes sense once you understand the motives behind them. Of critical importance to the buyer in an SPA is that he is assured that he is buying all of the stock or equity in the company. He or she will require the seller to make representations that the seller actually owns all of the stock of the company; that no other parties (say, a divorced spouse) will have any claims on equity in the company; and that the stock was issued properly. The buyer is also likely to require representations about the company's financial statements, any possible litigation, and the lack of a "material adverse effect" on the company's business.

Conversely, the seller typically seeks to limit the scope of the representations and warranties to include only those regarding the power and authority to enter into the transaction and the ownership of the stock. The seller may limit the representations by using knowledge qualifiers ("to the Seller's knowledge, there is no...") and materiality qualifiers ("the Seller has good and valid title to all the Purchased Assets, in all material respects..."). The buyer, on the other hand, typically provides limited representations and warranties as to its corporate power and authority to enter into the transaction and the sufficiency of its funds to complete the purchase.

In both an APA and an SPA, the seller also agrees to pre-closing covenants to continue to operate the business in the ordinary course and to pay debts and liabilities as they become due. The seller and buyer agree to work together toward closing and to share certain information. The buyer may ask that the seller agree to a non-compete provision, prohibiting the seller from competing with the buyer, or a non-solicitation provision, prohibiting the seller from soliciting employees or customers, each following the closing. You can see why there is a lot of negotiation in this part of the purchase agreement, can't you?

ESCROW AND INDEMNIFICATION

As a result of the potentially contentious issues arising from reps & warranties, buyers and sellers have traditionally been conflicted on how transaction-related risks should be shared between them. The purchaser seeks security and protection in the event of post-closing breaches of representation and warranties, while the seller wants a clean exit with as few post-closing obligations.

Historically (and still valid today although at a diminishing rate), a buyer would look to implement an escrow or other holdback of a portion of the purchase price for a fixed period of time which could be used in the event of a claim against the seller. Naturally, the seller was sensitive to such hold-back as it meant less cash for them at closing.

Good news then that in recent years an insurance innovation known as representation and warranty insurance has emerged to address this issue. "RWI" essentially shifts the financial risk for breaches of reps and warranties to an insurance company which enables the sellers to receive the full purchase price proceeds at closing and the buyer to be indemnified for losses resulting from a breach of representations and warranties by the seller.

According to the American Bar Association, the percentage of transactions expressly referencing RWI as a component of the M&A transactions increased from 29% in 2017 to 52% in their 2019 study.

RWI protects the buyer from losses resulting from inaccuracies in the reps and warranties made by the seller in the purchase agreement and reduces/eliminates the need for any of the traditional methods applied for managing such risk in M&A transactions (such as escrow or other holdback of a portion of the purchase price, third-party guaranties, and other contractual protections).

RWI premium is a function of the amount of coverage—typically 3–4% of the insured amount with a nonrefundable underwriting fee usually between $25,000-$50,000 USD.

A quick reminder of key items to bear in mind during negotiations:

- **Escrow Amount:** Many transactions require an 8% to 20% "holdback" of the purchase price in escrow for potential claims against ordinary representations and warranties that may arise after closing.

- **Survival Period:** This is the period of time buyers are allowed to make claims against the seller's ordinary representations and warranties (typically 12 to 24 months).

- **Indemnification Threshold:** A minimum level of potential losses from claims made by the buyer before making a claim against the escrow. Having a threshold of 10% to 20% of the escrow amount can help avoid minor post-closing disputes.

- **Indemnification Limits:** Typically, the amount that the buyer can claim from the seller is capped at 20% to 40% of the purchase price. Often, a buyer will require that losses from certain activities, such as fraud or intentional misrepresentation, criminal activity, etc., will not be capped. When buyers have identified specific risk areas during due diligence (such as questionable tax structuring of certain transactions), they will ask the seller to remove the cap for those issues as well.

COORDINATING SCHEDULES AND AVAILABILITY

You should assume that on the day of signing the purchase agreement, someone key to the process will be traveling, often in a foreign country. It just seems to work out that way. It's crucial, therefore, to coordinate in advance the calendars of those who will be signing the documents. If any necessary individual (i.e., fellow shareholders in your firm) is going to be traveling, secure his or her signatures in advance, to be held in escrow, along with clear instructions on how their signatures will be released. This may also include officers within your company whose signature might be essential on a minor document included in the definitive agreement. (Remember that checklist? If you manage it correctly, it will help you see a problem like this coming.)

The managing members or officers will be aware of their requirement to sign documents and be available throughout the day of the closing, but the company secretary, for example, who might not otherwise be involved in the transaction or even on-site on a regular basis, may be required to sign just one certificate. Be sure that they will be available on the day, or get that signature ahead of time.

CONFIRM ALL WIRE TRANSFER INSTRUCTIONS

The sale of your business almost certainly involves a lot of money. It seems like common sense to confirm—and reconfirm, and triple-confirm—that everyone has the right wire transfer instructions. Yet you'd be surprised how many people wait until the day of closing to check on this. If there is a foreign exchange element to contend with, i.e., your buyer is paying the funds into a foreign account, for example, do your homework well in advance to ensure you are using a credible F/X service that offers you the most advantageous exchange rates. The difference can add up to a significant amount. Avoid the stress and maintain a greater sense of control over the process by confirming such details long in advance. Once you've confirmed these details, it's worthwhile to confirm via e-mail that the buyer received them—and that your deal team confirms that they are correct on any relevant document where such details are listed.

CHAPTER 11

AFTER THE SALE

*"It is one of the most beautiful compensations in life
that no man can sincerely try to help another without helping himself."*

—Ralph Waldo Emerson

One of the payoffs of a successful sale is, quite literally, money. Sometimes it's a great deal of money. Paradoxically, this thing we strive so hard for can also be our undoing.

I learned this firsthand from a client as we had coffee one day in London's Leicester Square. After selling his first business nearly a decade earlier, he had called the local newspaper to give them a story about his success, so everyone would know. Then he descended into a world of drugs, alcohol, and what he called, with a bit of dark humor, "too much excess." It had literally been a dangerous time. "It nearly killed me," he said.

I was there to help him sell his next business, and he knew he needed to proceed differently. He retained a private wealth manager who helped him plan for and manage his success. When the sale was complete, the manager paid off all my client's debts, then spent time with him to understand how he wanted to support his son, a young adult, in his own endeavors. They developed a system of financial vehicles, including a trust for his son, which protected his assets against any sort of lawsuit and minimized his tax liabilities. With his personal financial picture in balance, he turned his attention to charitable work. And he kept a low profile about his success.

Somebody once said that life is not about having no problems, it's about which problems you choose to have. By going through the successful sale of your business, you have made a conscious decision to exchange one problem set for another. Thriving in this new world you have made means grappling effectively with these new problems.

For instance, if you have collected a substantial sum of money, I promise that you will face some potentially awkward conversations. Perhaps your old friends are treating you a bit differently. Maybe they even make a remark about how "you should pick up the tab" (especially if you've publicized your success). Or you have fielded awkward inquiries from family members who would like a loan or a gift.

The owners I have helped have wanted to do many things—start another business, travel, buy a blue water sailboat, launch a charity, fund their grandchildren's education. All of them, however, have taken the time to do careful follow-on work. I have seen commonalities among those who handled their successful exit well. If they earn a substantial sum of money through sale, they retain a wealth advisor to help them be strategic around using that money. They tend to maintain, more or less, the same lifestyle they lived before. If they are younger, they turn their attention quickly to their next endeavor. If they are ready to retire, they focus on their families and charitable work.

You didn't get to this point by accident. You got here through care, focus, and discipline. I'm not an expert in post-sale psychology, but if I have any advice to give, it's "don't stop now!" Just as you planned for your business, and as you planned for the sale of your business, plan for what comes next.

When you first engaged in exit planning, I suggested that your team include a wealth advisor. That individual should have worked with you all through the sales process. He or she should help you understand the financial implications of various choices you face so that you could make the best decisions. (See Chapter 5 for more details.)

Regardless of how you choose to address it, your problem set now includes navigating the world of wealth management. That subject is, frankly, not my specialty, and this book is not designed to give you in-depth advice on how to do that. However, as part of the process of selling your business, you would do well to think about what will be on your plate after the sale—to think about your new problem set.

Here's a very high-level summary of things you may want to consider and consult a wealth advisor about before, during, and after the sale of your business.

There are some big considerations right off the bat:

- Income tax issues
- Investment, retirement, and wealth transfer planning
- Changing insurance needs

Start planning for these before you close on the sale. Going forward, the things you should be thinking about can be grouped roughly into three buckets. Plan to have extensive and ongoing conversations with your wealth advisor about these:

- Investment management
- Charitable giving
- Dynastic planning

Investment management encompasses keeping and growing your wealth. You'll want to consider diversification, asset management, cash flow planning, and debt management, as well as ongoing tax planning.

Charitable giving includes the timing of charitable gifts (which can have significant tax implications), and consideration of formal structures for giving—for example, charitable trusts or family foundations.

Dynastic planning concerns the relationship between you, your money, and the rest of your family. This can be defined through your will, your medical plans, and your power of attorney; plans for regular gift giving to family members (which is potentially tax-advantaged); setting up trusts to transfer wealth; or the creation of a professionally run family office to manage all of your financial matters. There are also more immediate concerns, such as prenuptial agreements, allowances, and paying for children's educations.

***

AN IMPORTANT FINAL NOTE TO ENTREPRENEURS EVERYWHERE (FROM MARK CARMICHAEL)

This book has been about learning the rules before you get in the game as they relate to planning, marketing, selling, and the successful conclusion of a crucial event in your life: the sale of your company.

I've done my best to share actionable, honest insights and to be clear about my biases as I did so. My desire is that by this point you feel more equipped, empowered and confident in your ability to effectively engage in the process of planning for the sale of your business, and that however you proceed, you will consider yourself prepared to ask the right questions, make high-quality decisions, avoid the pitfalls, and navigate to your most successful exit.

On a personal note, it has been my privilege to aid you in preparing for your eventual exit. This book is the result of a distinctive set of principles I've acquired, refined and applied to countless exit processes since 2006, working with business owners around the world, selling businesses big and small, in just about every industry and geography imaginable.

Every business owner should be aware of these "rules" and adopt them in their respective exits—but most don't...or won't. Instead, they'll make the decision to embark upon the exit journey uninformed. And this leads to poor decision-making which all-too-often results in failure to sell.

It's my hope that your successful exit will start with learning the rules first; then determining the right path—or roadmap—to be followed which poses the highest probability of your successful outcome.

As someone who has been down this road many times before, my door is always open should you need any assistance, resources or an unbiased party to talk to. I am passionate about the entrepreneurial journey and as such, am always happy to be useful to others however I can. You can reach out to me at *ExitSupport@markcarmichael.com*.

I wish you every success in your exit journey and congratulate you for taking the initiative to become more informed and empowered in this respect. Tomorrow's successful exits belong to those who prepare for them today.

***

You may also find **The Exit Academy** to be of significant value to you. It's my 11½ hour online, on-demand video course on how to develop, implement and execute the most effective strategy for selling your business. It's an extension of this book and goes in depth on each stage of the selling process, following my Selling-Your-Business Roadmap™ which is designed to empower, educate and motivate entrepreneurs on achieving their exit.

And finally, I encourage you to reach out to me directly if you're seriously contemplating the sale of your business. My firm, STS Capital Partners, specializes in guiding entrepreneurs around the world on their individual paths to an exceptional exit. We typically work with entrepreneur and family-owned businesses valued in excess of $50 million, but occasionally advise businesses with values below this amount (and often with businesses exceeding $500 million in value). If you'd like to speak confidentially, you can do so by emailing me at ExitSupport@markcarmichael.com. I'll spare you the sales pitch; instead, we can talk about your business, your exit objectives, the areas that are keeping you awake at night and what you can expect (and look out for) in your own journey to exit. If we both feel there's a fit, then we can talk about how we might work together. Until that point though, you can view me as a trusted friend whose been down this path many times before you and who is happy to share his experiences, resources, knowledge and passion with you on all things exit-related.

You can learn more by visiting *www.markcarmichael.com*

ABOUT THE AUTHOR :
MARK CARMICHAEL

Mark Carmichael is a global thought leader on the topic of selling privately owned businesses. Today, he and his firm, STS Capital Partners, are highly regarded as one of the world's leading M&A advisory firms, guiding entrepreneurs on their respective business exits. He has an unwavering commitment to empower and inform business owners on the central principles that influence how businesses are most effectively marketed and sold in today's world.

Now in its 2nd Edition, *The Intelligent Exit* book has received international recognition in the category of Best Business Book. To further reinforce his mission in preparing business owners for successful exits, Mark recently created and launched **The Exit Academy**, an 11½ hour on-demand, online video training course for entrepreneurs on how to develop, implement and execute exit strategies designed to maximize the probability of extraordinary exits in today's world.

An MBA graduate of Oxford University, Mark is an international corporate finance deal-maker, university guest speaker, public speaker, and an entrepreneurial junkie.

An American by birth, Mark currently lives in Amsterdam, The Netherlands with his wife Marije, and their children, Maximilian, Mason and Amelia. His clients range from software companies to gold mines, consumer packaged goods to cryptocurrency exchanges and virtually every type of business in between. He and his team regularly work with private and family-owned businesses from around the world with valuations (typically) between 50m-500m (USD, EUR).

You can learn more about Mark, STS Capital Partners, **The Exit Academy** and how to work together with Mark at ***www.markcarmichael.com***.

As a reader of *The Intelligent Exit*, you are welcome to reach out to Mark and his team directly at ***mcarmichael@stscapital.com*** with any questions you may have on your own exit journey. Our door is always open and we're happy to add value however we can; whether it's advice, feedback or just to have an open discussion with an unbiased expert in the field of selling businesses, we encourage you to reach out.

***

Printed in Great Britain
by Amazon

10775062R00129